PALESTINE

Scale of miles

0   10   20   30   40

MEDITERRANEAN SEA

Sidon

PHOENICIA

Tyre

Leontes

Mt. Lebanon

Damascus

Mt. Hermon

ITUREA

Caesarea-Philippi

River

GALILEE

Capernaum

Genesaret

Bethsaida

Magdala

Dalmanutha

Tiberias

Mt. of Beatitudes

Nazareth

Cana of

Galilee

Mt. Thabor

Plain of Esdraelon

Naim

Bethsaida-Julias

Gergesa

Sea of Galilee

Gadara

DECAPOLIS

Scythopolis

SAMARIA

Enon

Samaria

Sichem Sichar

Plain of Sharon

Gerasa

Jordan River

R. Jabbok

PEREA

Ephrem

Jericho

JUDEA

Emmaus

JERUSALEM

Bethlehem

Bethany (Bethania)

Brook Cedron

Bethany (Bethabara)

Hebron

DESERT OF JUDEA

DEAD SEA

Machaerus

IDUMEA

THE JOURNEYS OF JESUS

COMPILED FROM
THE GOSPEL NARRATIVE

BOOK TWO

SISTER JAMES STANISLAUS
OF THE SISTERS OF ST. JOSEPH OF CARONDELET
ST. LOUIS, MISSOURI

WITH ILLUSTRATIONS AFTER BIDA

ST. AUGUSTINE ACADEMY PRESS
HOMER GLEN, ILLINOIS

Nihil Obstat

STI. LUDOVICI, DIE 8 NOVEMBRIS 1927

JOANNES ROTHENSTEINER
CENSOR LIBRORUM

Imprimatur

STI. LUDOVICI, DIE 9 NOVEMBRIS 1927

✠ JOANNES J. GLENNON
ARCHIEPISCOPUS
STI. LUDOVICI

This book was originally published in 1928
by Ginn and Company.

This facsimile edition was reproduced in 2025
by St. Augustine Academy Press.

ISBN: 978-1-64051-133-0

PREFACE

Book Two of "The Journeys of Jesus" is a continuation of the record of the events of the Public Ministry of Jesus begun in Book One of the series. This volume includes four of the ten Journeys, and relates the incidents that took place during the third year of Our Lord's Public Ministry.

Each event as narrated in the Gospel during this period forms a distinct topic in one chapter, given in the words of the New Testament. The descriptions of places and buildings at the ends of the chapters have been gathered from reliable sources. At the end of each narrative questions on the text are included.

Maps and numerous illustrations form an attractive feature of the books and serve to impress and make clearer the lesson of the printed page. A Biblical Glossary of names, with their pronunciations and definitions, is found at the end of the book.

The author wishes to express her deep appreciation and grateful acknowledgment to the B. Herder Book Company for permission to use the classification of places into journeys as given in the "Life of Jesus Christ," by A. J. Maas, of the Society of Jesus.

CONTENTS

THE THIRD YEAR OF THE PUBLIC MINISTRY OF JESUS

A SIXTH JOURNEY OF JESUS

CONTENTS

CONTENTS

[xi]

THE JOURNEYS OF JESUS

BOOK TWO

THE THIRD YEAR
OF THE PUBLIC MINISTRY OF JESUS

A SIXTH JOURNEY
OF JESUS

During this journey our Divine Saviour traveled through the land of Genesareth, and from thence to the cities of Tyre and Sidon. He returned by way of the Leontes and Jordan Rivers, going through Decapolis, and passed onward toward Magedan and Dalmanutha. From these towns He turned to the desert near Bethsaida, and thence northward to Cæsarea-Philippi. He came southward from there to Mount Thabor in Galilee; and from this mount He returned to Capharnaum, where He remained until the Feast of the Tabernacles.

The principal things to be remembered about this journey are:

The Reproof of the Pharisees
The True Defilement
The Cure of the Daughter of the Chanaanite Woman
The Cure of the Deaf-Mute
The Second Multiplication of Loaves
The Demand of the Pharisees
The Warning of the Leaven of the Pharisees
The Cure of a Blind Man

THE JOURNEYS OF JESUS

The Confession and Primacy of Peter
The First Prediction of the Passion
The Transfiguration on Mount Thabor
The Cure of a Demoniac Boy
The Cause of the Disciples' Failure
The Second Prediction of the Passion
The Payment of the Tribute
The Apostles' Dispute
The Discourse on Scandal
The Correction and Forgiveness of a Brother
The Parable of a King and his Servants

I

JESUS IN THE LAND OF GENESARETH

HE REPROVES THE PHARISEES

The Pharisees had a system of ablutions or cleansings about which they were very strict. St. Mark says that they were accustomed to wash their hands with the greatest care and to bathe the whole body on their return from any public place. They were forever cleansing their cups, water-jars, brazen pots, and the wooden parts of the couches upon which their guests reclined.

As Our Saviour disregarded many of these external observances and allowed His disciples to disregard them, the Pharisees and Scribes asked Jesus: "Why do Thy disciples transgress the tradition of the ancients? For they wash not their hands when they eat bread."

A severe rebuke was the only answer they received from the gentle Saviour. He asked them: "Why do you also transgress the commandment of God for your tradition? . . . Hypocrites, well hath Isaias prophesied of you, saying:

"This people honoreth Me with their lips: but their heart is far from Me.

"And in vain do they worship Me, teaching doctrines and commandments of men." (St. Matthew xv, 2–3, 7–9.)

This was the first time that Jesus was so severe in condemning the Pharisees because they put obedience to the teaching of their rabbis before obedience to the commands of God.

DEFILEMENT COMES FROM THE HEART

"And having called together the multitudes unto Him, He said to them: Hear ye and understand.

"Not that which goeth into the mouth defileth a man: but what cometh out of the mouth, this defileth a man.

"Then came His disciples, and said to Him: Dost Thou know that the Pharisees, when they heard this word, were scandalized?

"But He answering, said: Every plant which My heavenly Father hath not planted, shall be rooted up.

"Let them alone: they are blind, and leaders of the blind. And if the blind lead the blind, both fall into the pit.

"And Peter answering, said to Him: Expound to us this parable.

JESUS IN THE LAND OF GENESARETH

"But He said: Are you also yet without understanding?"

Then Our Lord went on to explain how the soul is defiled by the inward consent given to sin, saying:

"But the things which proceed out of the mouth, come forth from the heart, and those things defile a man.

"For from the heart come forth evil thoughts, murders, adulteries, fornications, thefts, false testimonies, blasphemies.

"These are the things that defile a man. But to eat with unwashed hands doth not defile a man." (St. Matthew xv, 10–20.)

QUESTIONS

1. Why did Jesus reprove the Pharisees?

2. At this time what did Jesus call these people?

3. What did Isaias prophesy of them?

4. Had Jesus before this time openly condemned them?

5. What is it that Jesus rewards most in all our good works?

6. What things, according to Our Lord's words, defile the soul of man?

II

JESUS IN THE PAGAN PROVINCES OF PHŒNICIA

HE HEALS THE DAUGHTER OF THE CHANAANITE WOMAN

The Pharisees were so angry with Jesus and tried so continuously to arouse the people against Him that He saw it would be impossible to remain in Galilee and accomplish any good work. And in Judea, "He would no longer walk there because the Jews sought to kill Him."

The people of Capharnaum had loved and honored Him, but at this time they had grown cold toward Him. Although they never treated Him with the bitter hatred that the people of Jerusalem displayed, still they had lost their first faith in Him. What was left to Jesus, then, but to turn toward the pagan territory of the northwest?

Phœnicia extended along the eastern shore of the Mediterranean from Carmel to Northern Lebanon. Its width varied from two to ten miles, and it was generally known by its two principal cities, Tyre,

JESUS IN THE PAGAN PROVINCES

then called the "Queen of the Seas," and Sidon. It is not likely that Jesus entered either of these cities, but instead He "went into the borders," for He desired to hide Himself from the multitude. St. Mark says, "He would that no man should know it."

But His coming could not continue entirely unnoticed, for His great works had long since been known to the people here. They had journeyed from Tyre and Sidon to hear His words and to beg Him to heal their sick.

As He was passing along a road near Tyre, a woman, very likely a Gentile of the upper class and well educated, who had heard of Christ the Prophet, hurried out of her house. Her daughter lay within, troubled by an unclean spirit. The woman cried to the Saviour: "Have mercy on me, O Lord, Thou Son of David: my daughter is grievously troubled by a devil."

Our Lord answered not a word. Without heeding His silence she followed Him and kept on begging His mercy. His disciples came and besought Him, saying: "Send her away, for she crieth after us."

And Jesus answering, said: "I was not sent but to the sheep that are lost of the house of Israel."

The woman was not discouraged by His seemingly harsh words, but, casting herself at the feet of Jesus, she adored Him, saying: "Lord, help me."

THE CHANAANITE WOMAN

JESUS IN THE PAGAN PROVINCES

Neither her tears nor her words seemed to move the Lord, and the disciples stood amazed. Probably this was the first time they had seen the tender heart of the Saviour remain untouched at the sight of tears.

Jesus said: "It is not good to take the bread of the children, and to cast it to the dogs.

"But she said: Yea, Lord: for the whelps also eat of the crumbs that fall from the table of their masters.

"Then Jesus answering, said to her: O woman, great is thy faith: be it done to thee as thou wilt: and her daughter was cured from that hour." (St. Matthew xv, 21–28.)

The Chanaanite woman hurried back to her house and there "she found the girl lying upon the bed, and that the devil was gone out." (St. Mark vii, 30.)

Our Saviour teaches us in this miracle the power of believing, persevering, and humble prayer.

TYRE AND SIDON

Tyre was the principal city of Phœnicia and was on the Mediterranean coast south of Sidon. Sidon was about twenty-seven miles north of Tyre, at the foot of Mount Lebanon and close to the Mediterranean coast. The two cities of Tyre and Sidon, until they were attacked by Assyria, were the most splendid and wealthy cities in the world.

[13]

QUESTIONS

1. Why did Jesus not remain in Galilee or Judea?

2. Locate on your map Phœnicia, Tyre, and Sidon.

3. Why did Jesus visit this pagan territory?

4. Had He ever visited these places?

5. How was it that He was known there?

6. Relate as much as you can of the story about the Phœnician woman and her daughter.

7. Was the woman a Jew or a Gentile?

8. What excellent qualities do we notice in her prayer?

III

JESUS IN DECAPOLIS

HE HEALS THE DEAF-MUTE

Jesus, leaving the coasts of Tyre, traveled by way of Sidon to the Sea of Galilee. He went first toward the north, then eastward, and through the valley of the Leontes, coming out near the source of the Jordan. He then turned His steps toward Decapolis. He was not entirely unknown in these cities, for the possessed persons of Gerasa had published His power (see "Journeys of Jesus, Book One," pp. 153-155).

"And they bring to Him one deaf and dumb; and they besought Him that He would lay His hand upon him.

"And taking him from the multitude apart, He put His fingers into his ears, and spitting, He touched his tongue:

"And looking up to heaven He groaned, and said to him: Ephpheta, which is, Be thou opened.

"And immediately his ears were opened, and the string of his tongue was loosed, and he spoke right.

[15]

JESUS HEALETH THE DEAF MAN

"And He charged them that they should tell no man. But the more He charged them, so much the more a great deal did they publish it.

"And so much the more did they wonder, saying: He hath done all things well; He hath made both the deaf to hear, and the dumb to speak." (St. Mark vii, 32–37.)

The Second Multiplication of Loaves

To avoid the multitudes the Divine Master retired into the wild desert highlands lying east of the Sea of Galilee. It was now sometime between May and September in the third year of His public teaching.

"And going up into a mountain, He sat there.

"And there came to Him great multitudes, having with them the dumb, the blind, the lame, the maimed, and many others: and they cast them down at His feet, and He healed them." (St. Matthew xv, 29–30.)

"And Jesus called together His disciples, and said: I have compassion on the multitudes, because they continue with me now three days, and have not what to eat, and I will not send them away fasting, lest they faint in the way.

"And the disciples say unto Him: Whence then should we have so many loaves in the desert, as to fill so great a multitude?

"And Jesus said to them: How many loaves have you? But they said: Seven, and a few little fishes.

"And He commanded the multitude to sit down upon the ground.

"And taking the seven loaves and the fishes, and giving thanks, He brake, and gave to His disciples, and the disciples gave to the people.

"And they did all eat, and had their fill. And they took up seven baskets full, of what remained of the fragments.

"And they that did eat, were four thousand men, beside children and women.

"And having dismissed the multitude, He went up into a boat, and came into the coasts of Magedan." (St. Matthew xv, 32–39.)

In this second multiplication of loaves Our Saviour prepared the minds of the people, and especially the minds of the Apostles, for the institution of the Holy Eucharist.

At the first multiplication of loaves (see "Journeys of Jesus, Book One," pp. 180–181) a boy carried the loaves; at the second, the disciples had the loaves. At the first there were two fishes; at the second, a few fishes. At the first, five loaves; at the second, seven loaves. At the first, twelve baskets of fragments were gathered up; at the second, seven baskets.

THE MIRACLE OF THE LOAVES AND FISHES

THE JOURNEYS OF JESUS

QUESTIONS

1. Compare the first and second multiplications of loaves under these heads:

People, Loaves, Fishes, Fragments.

2. In the two multiplications of loaves, for what was Jesus preparing the minds of the disciples and of the people?

IV

JESUS IN DALMANUTHA AND MAGEDAN

THE PHARISEES ASK FOR A SIGN

When the crowds had gone, Jesus, entering a boat, directed His Apostles to land, not at Capharnaum, but upon the shores of Magedan, or Magdala. About a mile south of Magedan was a valley called Dalmanutha. Between these two places Jesus landed, seeking retirement in a lonely spot.

But in spite of all the care He took to hide Himself, "there came to Him the Pharisees and Sadducees tempting: and they asked Him to show them a sign from heaven." They wished Him to give heavenly signs, such as Moses gave when he supplied their forefathers with bread from heaven.

"But He answered and said to them: When it is evening, you say, It will be fair weather, for the sky is red.

"And in the morning: To day there will be a storm, for the sky is red and lowering. You know then how to discern the face of the sky: and can you not know the signs of the times?

"A wicked and adulterous generation seeketh after a sign: and a sign shall not be given it, but the sign of Jonas the prophet. And He left them, and went away." (St. Matthew xvi, 1–4.)

What were the "signs of the times" which they could not, or would not, heed? Some of those foretold by the prophets were: the star at Christ's birth foretold by Moses (Numbers xxiv, 17); the "Voice from heaven" and the Dove descending upon Christ (St. Matthew iii, 16, 17); the testimony of John the Baptist (St. John i, 29); the sick and feeble healed; the dead raised to life; and the sceptre taken from Juda;—all of which signs had already been fulfilled.

Leaving the Pharisees, Jesus went again into the boat and sailed northward, quitting the shores of Galilee, which He was to visit but once more and that as secretly as possible, before He turned toward Jerusalem.

QUESTIONS

1. After the multiplication of loaves Jesus directed His Apostles to set sail for what place?

2. Why did He choose this lonely place?

3. Who came to Him here?

4. What did they wish of Him?

5. Did He give them what they asked? Why?

6. What did He give them?

7. Who were the Sadducees and Pharisees?

8. Tell the story of Jonas.

THE WARNING AGAINST THE LEAVEN
OF THE PHARISEES

At the command of Jesus, the Apostles drew away from the land and set sail for the northern part of the lake. In the haste of their departure they had forgotten to take bread. And they had but one loaf with them on the ship.

As they were grieving over their neglect, Jesus spoke to them in words which were meant to turn their thoughts away from earthly cares. He said: "Take heed and beware of the leaven of the Pharisees and Sadducees.

"But they thought within themselves, saying: Because we have taken no bread.

"And Jesus knowing it, said: Why do you think within yourselves, O ye of little faith, for that you have no bread?

"Do you not yet understand, neither do you remember the five loaves among five thousand men, and how many baskets you took up?

"Nor the seven loaves among four thousand men, and how many baskets you took up?

"Why do you not understand that it was not concerning bread I said to you: Beware of the leaven of the Pharisees and Sadducees?

"Then they understood that He said not that they should beware of the leaven of bread, but of the doctrine of the Pharisees and Sadducees." (St. Matthew xvi, 6–12.)

QUESTIONS

1. What did Jesus mean by the "leaven of the Pharisees and Sadducees"?

2. Upon this occasion, in what way had Our Saviour reason to be disappointed in His disciples?

3. Why did He call them "Ye of little faith"?

V

JESUS NEAR BETHSAIDA-JULIAS

He Cures a Blind Man

The morning of the next day they reached land in the kingdom of Philip, and walked along the bank of the Jordan until they arrived at Bethsaida-Julias near where the Jordan flows into the Lake of Genesareth. Here some people, seeing Jesus, brought "to Him a blind man, and they besought Him that He would touch him.

"And taking the blind man by the hand, He led him out of the town; and spitting upon his eyes, laying His hands on him, He asked him if he saw any thing.

"And looking up, he said: I see men as it were trees, walking.

"After that again He laid His hands upon his eyes, and he began to see, and was restored, so that he saw all things clearly.

"And He sent him into his house, saying: Go into thy house, and if thou enter into the town, tell nobody." (St. Mark viii, 22–26.)

JESUS LEADETH THE BLIND MAN

JESUS NEAR BETHSAIDA–JULIAS

QUESTIONS

1. Where did this cure of a blind man take place?

2. Point to the place on the map.

3. Do you think that this man was blind from birth?

4. Quote words to prove your statement.

5. Can you give a reason why Jesus told the man to "tell nobody" of his miraculous cure?

VI

JESUS AT CÆSAREA-PHILIPPI

THE CONFESSION AND PRIMACY OF PETER

Shortly after this miracle, Jesus left Bethsaida-Julias, accompanied only by His Apostles. None of the inhabitants of the town followed. Jesus traveled northward past Lake Merom and arrived at Cæsarea-Philippi, so called by the tetrarch Philip in honor of Tiberius Cæsar, who was his protector.

While on the way to this city Our Lord asked His Apostles: "Whom do men say that the Son of Man is?"

The Apostles sorrowfully answered that no one in Israel had acknowledged Jesus to be the Messias. They said: "Some John the Baptist, and other some Elias, and others Jeremias, or one of the prophets."

Jesus had asked what the *people* said of Him, and received the answer. Now He put the same question to the Apostles: "But whom do *you* say that I am?"

This was a test of their faith. Simon Peter instantly took up the word, and, addressing Jesus, said: "Thou art Christ, the Son of the living God."

"THOU ART PETER; AND UPON THIS ROCK I WILL BUILD
MY CHURCH"

THE JOURNEYS OF JESUS

Receiving this confession of faith from the lips of His Apostle, Jesus said to him: "Blessed art thou, Simon Bar-Jona: because flesh and blood hath not revealed it to thee, but My Father Who is in heaven.

"And I say to thee: That thou art Peter; and upon this rock I will build My Church, and the gates of hell shall not prevail against it.

"And I will give to thee the keys of the Kingdom of Heaven. And whatsoever thou shalt bind upon earth, it shall be bound also in heaven: and whatsoever thou shalt loose on earth, it shall be loosed also in heaven." (St. Matthew xvi, 13–19.)

QUESTIONS

1. Where did Jesus and His disciples go from Bethsaida-Julias?

2. Locate the city on the map.

3. When alone with His Apostles, what did Jesus ask them?

4. When He received their answer, what did He again ask them?

5. Who gave an answer to this second question?

6. Quote the Apostle's answer.

7. What reward did Jesus give to this Apostle?

8. What four distinct promises did Jesus give concerning the Church?

JESUS AT CÆSAREA-PHILIPPI

THE FIRST PREDICTION OF THE PASSION

Jesus had strictly charged His Apostles to tell no man that He was Jesus, the Christ. Since the Apostles now believed that He was the Messias foretold by the prophets, "Jesus began to show His disciples, that He must go to Jerusalem, and suffer many things from the ancients and Scribes and chief priests, and be put to death, and the third day rise again."

And Peter, moved by love for His Master, Who had promised him the Primacy in the Church, and distressed by His talk of suffering and death, taking Him aside, said to Him: "Lord, be it far from Thee, this shall not be unto Thee."

Poor, hasty Peter! His love for the Master and his knowledge of the power of Jesus moved him to speak thus to Him; but Peter's was a human love and a human faith. Peter, knowing that he and the other Apostles were the courageous children of a warlike race, perhaps meant to resist by force the enemies of Jesus.

But Jesus, turning, rebuked Peter, saying: "Go behind Me, Satan, thou art a scandal unto Me: because thou savorest not the things that are of God, but the things that are of men." (St. Matthew xvi, 21–23.)

[31]

THE JOURNEYS OF JESUS

WHAT SHALL IT PROFIT A MAN?

While Peter stood there humbled and silent, Jesus called together His disciples and said: "If any man will come after Me, let him deny himself, and take up his cross, and follow Me.

"For he that will save his life, shall lose it: and he that shall lose his life for My sake, shall find it." (St. Matthew xvi, 24–25.)

"For what shall it profit a man, if he gain the whole world, and suffer the loss of his soul?

"Or what shall a man give in exchange for his soul?

"For he that shall be ashamed of Me, and of My words, in this adulterous and sinful generation: the Son of Man also will be ashamed of him, when He shall come in the glory of His Father with the holy angels." (St. Mark viii, 36–38.)

QUESTIONS

1. Upon what occasion did Jesus first predict His Passion?

2. How did Peter act when he heard this prediction?

3. At the time of this first prediction of the Passion, did Jesus give any hint of His Resurrection?

4. Quote the words in which the promise of the Resurrection is given.

VII

JESUS ON MOUNT THABOR

THE TRANSFIGURATION

Our Lord chose for His glorious Transfiguration Mount Thabor in Galilee. This mountain lies in the northeast corner of the plain of Esdraelon, east of Nazareth. The top of the mountain is flat and table-like. From this summit one has a magnificent view over the Mediterranean Sea, the Sea of Galilee, and a wide stretch of country.

It was while they were in the city of Cæsarea-Philippi that the Master had told His Apostles of His bitter Passion and Death. The news had plunged their souls into the deepest sorrow. But He was about to give to three of His Apostles a glimpse of His heavenly power and majesty.

"And after six days Jesus taketh unto Him Peter and James, and John his brother, and bringeth them up into a high mountain apart:

"And He was transfigured before them. And His face did shine as the sun: and His garments became white as snow.

[33]

"And behold there appeared to them Moses and Elias talking with Him.

"And Peter answering, said to Jesus: Lord, it is good for us to be here: if Thou wilt, let us make here three tabernacles, one for Thee, and one for Moses, and one for Elias.

"And as he was yet speaking, behold a bright cloud overshadowed them. And lo, a Voice out of the cloud, saying: This is My beloved Son, in Whom I am well pleased: hear ye Him.

"And the disciples hearing, fell upon their face, and were very much afraid.

"And Jesus came and touched them: and said to them, Arise, and fear not.

"And they lifting up their eyes saw no one but only Jesus.

"And as they came down from the mountain, Jesus charged them, saying: Tell the vision to no man, till the Son of Man be risen from the dead.

"And His disciples asked Him, saying: Why then do the Scribes say that Elias must come first?

"But He answering, said to them: Elias indeed shall come, and restore all things.

"But I say to you, that Elias is already come, and they knew him not, but have done unto him whatsoever they had a mind. So also the Son of Man shall suffer from them.

JESUS ON MOUNT THABOR

"Then the disciples understood, that He had spoken to them of John the Baptist." (St. Matthew xvii, 1–13.)

QUESTIONS

1. Locate Mount Thabor on the map, and give a short description of the mountain.

2. Which of the Apostles did Jesus take to the top of this mountain?

3. Why did He take these three?

4. Read the story of Moses and that of Elias. Can you find any reasons why they appeared with Jesus?

5. What was the purpose of the Transfiguration?

6. Have we any reason to think, from the words of the text, that the Transfiguration took place at night?

7. What did St. Peter wish to do when he saw Jesus, Moses, and Elias on the mountain?

8. What command did Jesus give to the three disciples concerning the vision?

9. Where did Jesus tell the Apostles of His approaching Passion?

VIII

JESUS AT THE FOOT OF MOUNT THABOR

A DEMONIAC BOY

On the day following His Transfiguration, when Our Lord and the Apostles to whom He had shown Himself transfigured came down from the mountain, they found a great crowd of people surrounding the rest of the Apostles, while some Scribes disputed with them.

The Gospel tells us that when Our Lord appeared at the foot of Mount Thabor with Peter, James, and John "all the people seeing Jesus, were astonished and struck with fear." Why this should be so we are not told by the Evangelist, but it may be that on the face of our Divine Saviour there still lingered some traces of the heavenly majesty of His Transfiguration.

The people's fear was very short, however, for St. Mark tells us that they ran to Him and saluted Him.

"And He asked them: What do you question about among you?

JESUS AT THE FOOT OF MOUNT THABOR

"And one of the multitude, answering, said: Master, I have brought my son to Thee, having a dumb spirit,

"Who, wheresoever he taketh him, dasheth him, and he foameth, and gnasheth with the teeth, and pineth away; and I spoke to Thy disciples to cast him out, and they could not.

"Who answering them, said: O incredulous generation, how long shall I be with you? how long shall I suffer you? bring him unto Me.

"And they brought him. And when he had seen Him, immediately the spirit troubled him; and being thrown down upon the ground, he rolled about foaming.

"And He asked his father: How long time is it since this hath happened unto him? But he said: From his infancy:

"And oftentimes hath he cast him into the fire and into waters to destroy him. But if Thou canst do any thing, help us, having compassion on us.

"And Jesus saith to him: If thou canst believe, all things are possible to him that believeth.

"And immediately the father of the boy crying out, with tears said: I do believe, Lord: help my unbelief.

"And when Jesus saw the multitude running together, he threatened the unclean spirit, saying to him: Deaf and dumb spirit, I command thee, go out of him; and enter not any more into him.

"And crying out, and greatly tearing him, he went out of him, and he became as dead, so that many said: He is dead.

"But Jesus taking him by the hand, lifted him up; and he arose." (St. Mark ix, 15–26.)

THE CAUSE OF THE DISCIPLES' FAILURE

"Then came the disciples to Jesus secretly, and said: Why could not we cast him out?"

Some time before, Jesus had predicted His approaching death, and because of this, their faith in Him had weakened. Now the Master in His answer to their question let them know this. "Jesus said to them: Because of your unbelief. For, amen I say to you, if you have faith as a grain of mustard seed, you shall say to this mountain, Remove from hence hither, and it shall remove; and nothing shall be impossible to you.

"But this kind is not cast out but by prayer and fasting." (St. Matthew xvii, 18–20.)

QUESTIONS

1. When Jesus and the three Apostles came down to the foot of the mountain, what dispute was being held?

JESUS AT THE FOOT OF MOUNT THABOR

2. Why were all "astonished and struck with fear" when Jesus appeared?

3. What did they answer when Jesus asked, "What do you question about among you"?

4. Had the father of the afflicted boy a strong faith in Christ's power?

5. Why did he say to Jesus, "I do believe, Lord: help my unbelief"?

6. What miracle did Jesus perform for the father of the boy?

7. Why had the disciples failed to cure the boy?

IX

JESUS ON THE WAY TO CAPHARNAUM

THE SECOND PREDICTION OF THE PASSION

Leaving Thabor, the Mount of Transfiguration, Jesus and His disciples took a roundabout way to reach Capharnaum. It led through quiet places of Galilee, for Jesus did not wish to attract further attention nor give occasion for any excitement or display of admiration.

The journey was made in secret. The Gospel tells us: "He would not that any man should know it."

It was on this journey that Jesus said to His disciples: "The Son of Man shall be betrayed into the hands of men:

"And they shall kill Him, and the third day He shall rise again."

The Apostles understood nothing of what He told them about His Passion, yet they did not question Him.

These words of the Master must have disturbed them greatly. The Gospel tells us that "they were troubled exceedingly." (St. Matthew xvii, 21–22.)

X

JESUS IN CAPHARNAUM

The Tribute Money

There were in Capharnaum some faithful souls, but the reception given to Christ and His Apostles on this occasion was very different from the receptions of former days. This was to be the last visit of Jesus to His adopted home. We can well imagine how He felt when, entering the town, He met coldness, even hostility, from the inhabitants.

The Master and His little band walked through the streets almost unnoticed by the passers-by. The tax-gatherers alone observed the group and, coming to Peter, said to him: "Doth not your master pay the didrachmas?" Peter, without reflection, immediately answered "Yes."

This didrachma was a sum of money which every Israelite, from his twentieth year upwards, had to pay to defray the expenses of the Temple. It was therefore a tribute to God. It amounted to about thirty-three cents of our money, and was usually paid in the month of March. Jesus had been absent from

Capharnaum almost six months, and it was now autumn, so that the time for payment had passed. Priests, Levites, and rabbis were not required to pay the tax. Hitherto the people had regarded Jesus as a "Doctor of the Law," and for this, if for no other reason, He also had been free from the tax.

Jesus Pays the Tribute Money

When Peter answered "Yes," it did not come to his mind that only a short time before he had said to Jesus: "Thou art Christ, the Son of the living God." As such our Blessed Lord was superior to all human overlordship, and free from all earthly taxation.

"And when he was come into the house, Jesus prevented him, saying: What is thy opinion, Simon? The kings of the earth, of whom do they receive tribute or custom? of their own children, or of strangers?

"And he said: Of strangers. Jesus said to him: Then the children are free.

"But that we may not scandalize them, go to the sea, and cast in a hook: and that fish which shall first come up, take: and when thou hast opened its mouth, thou shalt find a stater: take that, and give it to them for Me and thee." (St. Matthew xvii, 23–26.)

JESUS IN CAPHARNAUM

Jesus always obeyed just laws. He therefore paid the tribute, but He paid it as only God could do it, by a miracle. He thus proved His claim of exemption and yet His obedience to the law.

QUESTIONS

1. Why was Jesus exempt from taxes?

2. Since Jesus was not obliged to pay the tax, why did He pay it?

3. How did He secure the money to pay it?

4. Have Catholics any obligation to defray the expenses of the Church?

5. What is the fifth commandment of the Church?

THE APOSTLES' DISPUTE

On the way to Capharnaum, a dispute had arisen among the disciples as to which of them should be the greatest in the Kingdom of Heaven.

While they were in Capharnaum Jesus and His Apostles stayed with a family that believed in Him. It was here that Jesus gave His followers a lesson in humility.

"At that hour the disciples came to Jesus, saying: Who, thinkest Thou, is the greater in the Kingdom of Heaven?

"And Jesus calling unto Him a little child, set him in the midst of them,

[43]

JESUS AND A CHILD

JESUS IN CAPHARNAUM

"And said: Amen I say to you, unless you be converted, and become as little children, you shall not enter into the Kingdom of Heaven.

"Whosoever therefore shall humble himself as this little child, he is the greater in the Kingdom of Heaven.

"And he that shall receive one such little child in My Name, receiveth Me." (St. Matthew xviii, 1–5.)

QUESTIONS

1. How did Jesus settle the dispute among the Apostles as to which should have first place in the Kingdom of Heaven?

2. How were they to "become as little children"?

3. Why should we wish to "become as children"?

JESUS DISCOURSES ON SCANDAL

After Our Saviour had thus taught the Apostles not to be jealous of one another, His thoughts reached far into the future and He spoke further of the "little child" and the "weak one" who would be led astray by evil words and the bad example of others. He said:

"But he that shall scandalize one of these little ones that believe in Me, it were better for him that a millstone should be hanged about his neck, and that he should be drowned in the depth of the sea.

[45]

"Woe to the world because of scandals. For it must needs be that scandals come: but nevertheless woe to that man by whom the scandal cometh."

The great evil of the sin of scandal is shown by the terrific "woe" uttered against it by Our Saviour. He told the Apostles plainly what bodily evils should be suffered rather than that this sin be committed:

"And if thy hand, or thy foot scandalize thee, cut it off, and cast it from thee. It is better for thee to go into life maimed or lame, than having two hands or two feet, to be cast into everlasting fire.

"And if thy eye scandalize thee, pluck it out, and cast it from thee. It is better for thee having one eye to enter into life, than having two eyes to be cast into hell fire.

"See that you despise not one of these little ones: for I say to you, that their angels in heaven always see the face of My Father Who is in heaven." (St. Matthew xviii, 6–10.)

The Ninety-nine

The lesson which Our Lord constantly taught was that He had come on earth to save sinners. So, in this discourse with His disciples about the sin of scandal, He turned to speak about the sinner, and the desire of God that the sinner should be saved. He said:

JESUS IN CAPHARNAUM

"What think you? If a man have an hundred sheep, and one of them should go astray: doth he not leave the ninety-nine in the mountains, and go to seek that which is gone astray?

"And if it so be that he find it: Amen I say to you, he rejoiceth more for that, than for the ninety-nine that went not astray.

"Even so it is not the will of your Father, Who is in heaven, that one of these little ones should perish." (St. Matthew xviii, 12–14.)

On Brotherly Correction and Forgiveness

Earlier Jesus had spoken of everlasting fire as punishment for the sin of scandal. Now He taught His disciples of another "fire" which, once kindled, purifies all it touches. This is brotherly love. Jesus said:

"But if thy brother shall offend against thee, go, and rebuke him between thee and him alone. If he shall hear thee, thou shalt gain thy brother.

"And if he will not hear thee, take with thee one or two more: that in the mouth of two or three witnesses every word may stand.

"And if he will not hear them: tell the Church. And if he will not hear the Church, let him be to thee as the heathen and publican." (St. Matthew xviii, 15–17.)

[47]

THE JOURNEYS OF JESUS

In the beginning of the Church every Christian community was like a large family in which each member watched over and rejoiced in his brother's virtue. Those were days when the pagans wondered, and said of Christians: "Behold how they love one another."

Peter, hearing these rules of Christian love from the lips of the Saviour, said to Him: "Lord, how often shall my brother offend against me, and I forgive him? till seven times?"

The rabbis taught that to forgive three times was a great virtue. The Apostle Peter was much more indulgent than they, yet he was far from the infinite indulgence of the Master, Who answered his question with these words: "I say not to thee, till seven times; but till seventy times seven times." (St. Matthew xviii, 21–22.)

QUESTIONS

1. What can you say of the early Christians?

2. Why did the pagans wonder at them?

3. How many times does God forgive us our sins?

4. How often should we forgive those who offend us?

5. What class of people is meant by the word "ninety-nine" as it is used in this chapter?

6. What do you mean by the near occasions of sin?

7. Find out the meaning of scandal.

JESUS IN CAPHARNAUM

The King and his Two Servants

The better to impress the Apostles with His law of loving forgiveness, our Blessed Lord set before them this parable:

"Therefore is the Kingdom of Heaven likened to a king, who would take an account of his servants.

"And when he had begun to take the account, one was brought to him, that owed him ten thousand talents.

"And as he had not wherewith to pay it, his lord commanded that he should be sold, and his wife and children and all that he had, and payment to be made.

"But that servant falling down, besought him, saying: Have patience with me, and I will pay thee all.

"And the lord of that servant being moved with pity, let him go and forgave him the debt.

"But when that servant was gone out, he found one of his fellow servants that owed him an hundred pence: and laying hold of him, he throttled him, saying: Pay what thou owest.

"And his fellow servant falling down, besought him, saying: Have patience with me, and I will pay thee all.

"And he would not: but went and cast him into prison, till he paid the debt.

[49]

"Now his fellow servants seeing what was done, were very much grieved, and they came and told their lord all that was done.

"Then his lord called him; and said to him: Thou wicked servant, I forgave thee all the debt, because thou besoughtest me:

"Shouldst not thou then have had compassion also on thy fellow servant, even as I had compassion on thee?

"And his lord being angry, delivered him to the torturers until he paid all the debt.

"So also shall My heavenly Father do to you, if you forgive not every one his brother from your hearts." (St. Matthew xviii, 23–35.)

QUESTIONS

1. Relate the parable of the king and the two servants.

2. Can you give a reason why Christ related this parable?

3. "Forgive us our trespasses as we forgive those who trespass against us." Where are these words found?

4. When and by whom were they given to us?

A SEVENTH JOURNEY
OF JESUS

Jesus left Capharnaum sometime in September, to begin His seventh journey. He traveled southward through Galilee to Jerusalem, thence to Jericho, and across the Jordan to Bethany. Passing through the cities and towns of Perea, He turned again toward Jerusalem.

The principal things to be remembered about this journey are:

> The Refusal of Jesus to Go Publicly to the Feast
> The Feast of the Tabernacles
> The Samaritans' Refusal of Hospitality to Jesus
> The Teaching of Jesus in the Temple
> The Ceremony of Pouring the Waters of Siloe
> Nicodemus' Defense of Jesus before the Council
> The Pardon of the Sinful Woman
> The Cure of the Man Born Blind
> The Expulsion of the Man from the Temple
> The Parable of the Good Shepherd
> The Two Great Commandments
> The Parable of the Good Samaritan
> The Hospitality of Martha and Mary
> The Second Form of the Lord's Prayer
> The Value of Perseverance in Prayer

THE JOURNEYS OF JESUS

The Cure of a Dumb Man
The Sign of Jonas
The Mother of Jesus Called Blessed
The Pharisee's Banquet
The Warnings against Hypocrisy, Covetousness, and
    Worldly Care
The Watchful Servant
The Galileans Slain
The Barren Fig Tree
The Healing of the Crippled Woman
The Mustard Seed and the Leaven

XI

JESUS IN CAPHARNAUM

JESUS REFUSES TO GO PUBLICLY TO THE FEAST

The Feast of the Tabernacles was now at hand and the "brethren" of Jesus, that is, His relatives, said to Him: "Pass from hence, and go into Judea; that Thy disciples also may see Thy works which Thou dost.

"For there is no man that doth any thing in secret, and he himself seeketh to be known openly. If Thou do these things, manifest Thyself to the world.

"For neither did His brethren believe in Him." (St. John vii, 3–5.)

But Jesus knew that the time fixed by His heavenly Father for His death had not yet arrived. He also knew that at that time His Galilean disciples were so filled with enthusiasm over His wonderful deeds that they might attempt a public demonstration, and thus arouse the angry and stubborn opposition of the Jews against Him. This alone would hinder the work that He intended to do during the next six months.

Jesus said to His brethren: "My time is not yet come; but your time is always ready.

"The world cannot hate you; but Me it hateth: because I give testimony of it, that the works thereof are evil.

"Go you up to this festival day, but I go not up to this festival day: because My time is not accomplished.

"When He had said these things, He Himself stayed in Galilee" and let His kindred depart for Jerusalem without Him. (St. John vii, 6–9.)

THE FEAST OF THE TABERNACLES

The Feast of the Tabernacles, which usually took place in late September, or early in October, was the last in order of the three annual feasts at which the Jews were obliged to be present in Jerusalem. It had a twofold meaning: it was a feast of thanksgiving to the Lord for the harvest; and it was intended also to give Him thanks for leading the Jews for forty years through the desert, and bringing them at last to a land flowing with milk and honey.

During the celebration, which lasted seven days, the people lived under leafy booths woven of boughs, just as their fathers had lived in tents. The olive, the pine, the myrtle, and the palm trees were stripped of their branches for the purpose of building the booths. Streets, squares, level housetops, even the Court of the Gentiles, all were green with branches. Nothing was heard but songs of joy answering the blare of trumpets. Every Jew carried and waved either a palm branch, the symbol of victory, or a branch laden with rich fruit of the citron, which was considered the most beautiful of trees.

This rejoicing was all the more earnest because it followed the Feast of Expiation, which took place five days before. On the Feast of Expiation, the people observed a strict fast. The high priest offered in sacrifice two he-goats; one of these, being burdened with the sins of Israel, was driven forth into the desert, and was known as the "scapegoat." The Jews then considered themselves freed from sin, and in a proper mood to celebrate the great national Feast of the Tabernacles.

QUESTIONS

1. What two great religious feasts have just been mentioned?

2. Give a brief description of each.

3. Why did Jesus refuse to go publicly to the feast?

4. Why did His relatives wish Him to go?

5. Did they believe Him to be God?

XII

JESUS ON THE WAY TO JERUSALEM

THE SAMARITANS REFUSE HIM HOSPITALITY

Although Jesus had let His relatives go on to Jerusalem without Him, He decided to follow them. When He decided to do this, we are told by St. Luke that "He sent messengers before His face; and going, they entered into a city of the Samaritans, to prepare for Him.

"And they received Him not, because His face was of one going to Jerusalem."

(The Samaritans did not look upon Jerusalem as their holy place; hence their inhospitality to those who were going there to worship.)

"And when His disciples James and John had seen this, they said: Lord, wilt Thou that we command fire to come down from heaven, and consume them?

"And turnihg, He rebuked them, saying: You know not of what spirit you are.

"The Son of Man came not to destroy souls, but to save. And they went into another town." (St. Luke ix, 52–56.)

JESUS ON THE WAY TO JERUSALEM

QUESTIONS

1. What humiliation did Jesus receive at the beginning of His journey to Jerusalem?

2. Can you tell why the Samaritans did not receive Jews kindly?

3. Why did Jesus not punish them?

4. In what way did the conduct of the Apostles differ from that of Jesus?

5. Read the story of Elias and of the fire that he brought down from heaven.

THREE HALF-HEARTED FOLLOWERS OF JESUS

As the little group walked along the highway, a scribe, touched by the sight of the Saviour, came forward and said: "I will follow Thee whithersoever Thou goest."

The Lord heeded not his words, nor his rank as shown in his rich attire. The all-seeing eye of the Lord knew the scribe's great love for riches and the pleasures which riches could bring him. He also knew that the man's present fervor would lessen when he felt the poverty and sufferings of Jesus and His disciples. Therefore Jesus said to the scribe: "The foxes have holes, and the birds of the air nests; but the Son of Man hath not where to lay His head."

[57]

THE JOURNEYS OF JESUS

The same day, and upon the same highway, Jesus met a man who felt moved to follow Him, but who was grieved over the death of his father. The Searcher of hearts knew well this man's attachment to his home and family. Still, Jesus said to him: "Follow Me."

The man, surprised at the suddenness of the invitation, said to the Master: "Lord, suffer me first to go, and to bury my father."

Jesus had always taught that love and honor were due to parents; so He must have had good reasons for refusing this request. He replied: "Let the dead bury their dead: but go thou, and preach the Kingdom of God."

A third disciple on that day must have received the call of the Master too, for he said to Jesus: "I will follow Thee, Lord; but let me first take my leave of them that are at my house."

Jesus made answer: "No man putting his hand to the plough, and looking back, is fit for the Kingdom of God." (St. Luke ix, 57–62.)

QUESTIONS

1. Try to give a reason for the title of the section you have just read.

2. Tell some of the reasons that people give for not devoting themselves to the service of God.

3. Show that the words of Jesus were true in His own case: "The foxes have holes, and the birds of the air nests; but the Son of Man hath not where to lay His head."

4. Give in your own words the meaning of the last verse in this chapter.

5. Can you give a reason why the scribe, after offering to do so, did not follow Jesus?

6. Name a class of people who break away from every tie of love and affection to follow in the footsteps of Jesus.

7. In what way can you help the home and foreign missions?

8. When we are prompted to do a good work, is it safe to delay doing it?

XIII

JESUS IN JERUSALEM

He Teaches in the Temple

While Jesus was still on His way to Jerusalem, there was much talk about Him there. His absence had been noted, and on all sides was being discussed.

"The Jews therefore sought Him on the festival day, and said: Where is He?

"And there was much murmuring among the multitude concerning Him. For some said: He is a good man. And others said: No, but He seduceth the people.

"Yet no man spoke openly of Him, for fear of the Jews." (St. John vii, 11–13.)

Our Saviour entered Jerusalem while this whispering was still going on. "Now about the midst of the feast Jesus went up into the Temple, and taught." His presence there was a surprise to the people, and at first they listened to Him with attention and admiration, but He had not gone far in His instruction and explanations of the Old Testament when some prominent Jews broke the silence with muttered criticisms. They "wondered, saying: How doth this Man know letters, having never learned?

"Jesus answered them, and said: My Doctrine is not Mine, but His that sent Me.

"If any man will do the will of Him; he shall know of the doctrine, whether it be of God, or whether I speak of Myself.

"He that speaketh of himself, seeketh his own glory: but he that seeketh the glory of Him that sent him, he is true, and there is no injustice in him.

"Did not Moses give you the Law, and yet none of you keepeth the Law?"

Then Jesus, knowing their secret intention to kill Him, said to them: "Why seek you to kill Me?"

The leaders kept silent. The people in general did not know of the intention of the Jews to slay Jesus. They were shocked and amazed at His words, and, with insulting boldness, some of them said to Him: "Thou hast a devil; who seeketh to kill Thee?

"Jesus answered, and said to them: One work I have done; and you all wonder."

According to the Law of Moses, a good deed might be done on the Sabbath without breaking the Law. Jesus said: "Are you angry at Me because I have healed the whole man on the Sabbath day?

"Judge not according to the appearance, but judge just judgment." (St. John vii, 14–24.)

THE JOURNEYS OF JESUS

THE WATERS OF SILOE

Every morning during the seven days of the Feast of the Tabernacles a priest went down to the Fountain of Siloe which flowed at the foot of the holy mountain. In a golden vessel he drew water from the fountain. This water he carried back in solemn state to the Temple, and poured it on the altar, amidst the singing of psalms of thanksgiving for the harvest, and psalms in remembrance of the miraculous water which the Israelites had drunk in the desert. It is probable that this ceremony suggested the words of Jesus which we find in St. John's Gospel:

"And on the last, and great day of the festivity, Jesus stood and cried, saying: If any man thirst, let him come to Me, and drink.

"He that believeth in Me, as the Scripture saith, *Out of his belly shall flow rivers of living water.*

"Now this He said of the Spirit which they should receive, who believed in Him: for as yet the Spirit was not given, because Jesus was not yet glorified." (St. John vii, 37–39.)

The words of Jesus made a great impression on the multitude, for we are told that some said: "This is the Prophet indeed.

"Others said: This is the Christ. But some said: Doth the Christ come out of Galilee?

JESUS IN JERUSALEM

"Doth not the Scripture say: That Christ cometh of the seed of David, and from Bethlehem the town where David was?"

And we are told that "there arose a dissension among the people because of Him.

"And some of them would have apprehended Him: but no man laid hands upon Him." (St. John vii, 40–44.)

QUESTIONS

1. Quote the words of Jesus given in this chapter that refer to the Holy Spirit.

2. Which Person of the Blessed Trinity is the Holy Spirit?

3. Was it before or after the Resurrection of Our Lord that the Holy Spirit descended upon those who believed in Jesus?

4. What is the Sacrament of Confirmation?

5. What effect has it upon the souls of those who receive it worthily?

NICODEMUS DEFENDS JESUS BEFORE THE COUNCIL

"The ministers therefore came to the chief priests and the Pharisees. And they said to them: Why have you not brought Him?

"The ministers answered: Never did man speak like this Man.

"The Pharisees therefore answered them: Are you also seduced?

"Hath any one of the rulers believed in Him, or of the Pharisees?

"But this multitude, that knoweth not the law, are accursed.

"Nicodemus said to them (he that came to Him by night, who was one of them):

"Doth our law judge any man, unless it first hear him, and know what he doth?"

This defense of Jesus enraged the Great Council. They taunted Nicodemus with being a disciple of a Galilean, and they answered and said to him: "Art thou also a Galilean? Search the Scriptures, and see, that out of Galilee a prophet riseth not.

"And every man returned to his own house." (St. John vii, 45–53.)

QUESTIONS

1. How did Nicodemus try to defend Jesus before the Council? What were his words?

2. Was Jesus by birth a Galilean or a Judean?

3. Why did the Jews celebrate the Feast of the Tabernacles?

4. How did the words of our Divine Lord differ from those of other teachers of the Jews?

5. Why did the Jews insist that Our Lord was a Galilean?

JESUS IN JERUSALEM

The Sinful Woman

"And Jesus went unto Mount Olivet.

"And early in the morning He came again into the Temple, and all the people came to Him, and sitting down He taught them.

"And the Scribes and Pharisees bring unto Him a woman taken in adultery."

Moses had commanded the Jews to stone to death any one guilty of this sin, but the Romans had taken away from the Jews the right to put criminals to death. Nevertheless the Jews brought this woman to Jesus and said to Him: "Master, this woman was even now taken in adultery.

"Now Moses in the Law commanded us to stone such a one. But what sayest Thou?

"And this they said tempting Him, that they might accuse Him. But Jesus bowing Himself down, wrote with His finger on the ground.

"When therefore they continued asking Him, He lifted up Himself, and said to them: He that is without sin among you, let him first cast a stone at her.

"And again stooping down, He wrote on the ground."

We have no knowledge of what Jesus wrote. Some think that He wrote in the sand the secret sins of the woman's accusers.

THE WOMAN TAKEN IN ADULTERY

JESUS IN JERUSALEM

The Scribes and Pharisees, dumbfounded and silent, "went out one by one, beginning at the eldest." Soon there was left no one but Jesus "and the woman standing in the midst.

"Then Jesus lifting up Himself, said to her: Woman, where are they that accused thee? Hath no man condemned thee?" And she said to Him: "No man, Lord." Jesus once more showed His boundless love and mercy toward a poor fallen sinner, and said to her: "Neither will I condemn thee. Go, and now sin no more." (St. John viii, 1–11.)

QUESTIONS

1. Who only is without sin?

2. In what way was the Blessed Virgin without sin?

3. Before condemning others, what should each person do?

4. Is it a duty of anyone to condemn the sins and crimes of others?

5. Name such persons.

JESUS THE LIGHT OF THE WORLD

It was immediately after this incident that Jesus, seeing the extinguished torches which had been lighted for the Festival, spoke these words:

"I am the Light of the world: he that followeth

Me, walketh not in darkness, but shall have the light of life."

Some Pharisees who had mingled with the crowd, found fault with this saying of Jesus. They said: "Thou givest testimony of Thyself: Thy testimony is not true."

Jesus replied: "Although I give testimony of Myself, My testimony is true: for I know whence I came, and whither I go: but you know not whence I come, or whither I go.

"You judge according to the flesh: I judge not any man.

"And if I do judge, My judgment is true: because I am not alone, but I and the Father that sent Me.

"And in your Law it is written, that the testimony of two men is true.

"I am one that give testimony of Myself: and the Father that sent Me giveth testimony of Me."

The Pharisees greeted these words with shouts of mockery, and said: "Where is Thy Father?"

Jesus said to them: "Neither Me do you know, nor My Father: if you did know Me, perhaps you would know My Father also.

"These words Jesus spoke in the treasury, teaching in the Temple: and no man laid hands on Him, because His hour was not yet come." (St. John viii, 12–20.)

JESUS IN JERUSALEM

WHEN YOU SHALL HAVE LIFTED UP THE SON OF MAN

To the Jews Jesus said: "I go, and you shall seek Me, and you shall die in your sin. Whither I go, you cannot come."

Our Lord's many enemies among the Jews were now so set on putting Jesus to death that they thought it was impossible for Him to escape from their hands unless He killed Himself.

So they said: "Will He kill Himself, because He said: Whither I go, you cannot come?

"And He said to them: You are from beneath, I am from above. You are of this world, I am not of this world.

"Therefore I said to you, that you shall die in your sins. For if you believe not that I am He, you shall die in your sin.

"They said therefore to Him: Who art Thou? Jesus said to them: The Beginning, Who also speak unto you.

"Many things I have to speak and to judge of you. But He that sent Me, is true: and the things I have heard of Him, these same I speak in the world. . . .

"Jesus therefore said to them: When you shall have lifted up the Son of Man, then shall you know,

2 [69]

that I am He, and that I do nothing of Myself, but as the Father hath taught Me, these things I speak:

"And He that sent Me, is with Me, and He hath not left Me alone: for I do always the things that please Him.

"When He spoke these things, many believed in Him." (St. John viii, 21–30.)

QUESTION

Upon what occasion was the Son of Man lifted up?

JESUS HEALS THE MAN BLIND FROM HIS BIRTH

Jesus now went to a part of the city outside the Temple walls, where all was quiet. Walking along its streets He saw a man blind from his birth, who was begging. He stopped near him and cast on him a glance of heartfelt pity and compassion.

The sympathy of the Saviour aroused a similar feeling in the hearts of the disciples and they said: "Rabbi, who hath sinned, this man, or his parents, that he should be born blind?"

Jesus said to the disciples: "Neither hath this man sinned, nor his parents; but that the works of God should be made manifest in him.

"I must work the works of Him that sent Me, whilst it is day: the night cometh, when no man can work.

JESUS IN JERUSALEM

"As long as I am in the world, I am the Light of the world.

"When He had said these things, He spat on the ground, and made clay of the spittle, and spread the clay upon his eyes,

"And said to him: Go, wash in the pool of Siloe, which is interpreted, Sent."

The man did as Christ told him; he went and washed, and returned cured of his blindness. The people who had seen him begging were unwilling to believe him the same person. They said: "Is not this he that sat and begged?" Some said: "This is he," but others said: "No, but he is like him." But the man said: "I am he."

"They said therefore to him: How were thy eyes opened?

"He answered: That Man that is called Jesus made clay, and anointed my eyes, and said to me: Go to the pool of Siloe, and wash. And I went, I washed, and I see." (St. John ix, 1–11.)

IT WAS THE SABBATH

"They bring him that had been blind to the Pharisees.

"Now it was the Sabbath, when Jesus made the clay, and opened his eyes.

"Again therefore the Pharisees asked him, how he had received his sight. But he said to them: He put clay upon my eyes, and I washed, and I see.

"Some therefore of the Pharisees said: This Man is not of God, who keepeth not the Sabbath. But others said: How can a man that is a sinner do such miracles? And there was a division among them.

"They say therefore to the blind man again: What sayest thou of Him that hath opened thy eyes? And he said: He is a prophet.

"The Jews then did not believe concerning him, that he had been blind and had received his sight, until they called the parents of him that had received his sight,

"And asked them, saying: Is this your son, who you say was born blind? How then doth he now see?

"His parents answered them, and said: We know that this is our son, and that he was born blind:

"But how he now seeth, we know not; or who hath opened his eyes, we know not: Ask himself: He is of age, let him speak for himself.

"These things his parents said, because they feared the Jews: For the Jews had already agreed among themselves, that if any man should confess Him to be Christ, he should be put out of the synagogue.

"Therefore did his parents say: He is of age, ask himself.

JESUS IN JERUSALEM

"They therefore called the man again that had been blind, and said to him: Give glory to God. We know that this Man is a sinner.

"He said therefore to them: If He be a sinner, I know not: one thing I know, that whereas I was blind, now I see." (St. John ix, 13–25.)

How Did He Open thy Eyes?

So the Pharisees began again to question him. They said: "What did He to thee? How did He open thy eyes?"

He answered: "I have told you already, and you have heard: Why would you hear it again? will you also become His disciples?"

This angered them, and "they reviled him therefore and said: Be thou His disciple; but we are the disciples of Moses.

"We know that God spoke to Moses: but as to this Man, we know not from whence He is."

Not in the least terrified by their angry looks and words, the man said to them boldly: "Why, herein is a wonderful thing, that you know not from whence He is, and He hath opened my eyes.

"Now we know that God doth not hear sinners: but if a man be a server of God, and doth His will, him He heareth.

[73]

"From the beginning of the world it hath not been heard, that any man hath opened the eyes of one born blind.

"Unless this Man were of God, He could not do any thing."

At these words the Pharisees rose up in anger and cried out to the beggar: "Thou wast wholly born in sins, and dost thou teach us? And they cast him out."

When Jesus heard that they had cast the man out, He went in search of him. And when He had found him, He said to him: "Dost thou believe in the Son of God?"

"Who is He, Lord," answered the man, "that I may believe in Him?

"And Jesus said to him: Thou hast both seen Him; and it is He that talketh with thee.

"And he said: I believe, Lord. And falling down, he adored Him.

"And Jesus said: For judgment I am come into this world; that they who see not, may see; and they who see, may become blind.

"And some of the Pharisees, who were with Him, heard: and they said unto Him: Are we also blind?

"Jesus said to them: If you were blind, you should not have sin: but now you say: We see. Your sin remaineth." (St. John ix, 26–41.)

JESUS IN JERUSALEM

QUESTIONS

1. How did the Jews regard bodily infirmity?

2. In what words did Jesus make Himself known to the man born blind?

3. How did the Pharisees punish the man for acknowledging Christ as a prophet?

4. What virtue in the blind man merited his two-fold reward?

5. The blind man received his bodily sight. What else did he receive from Christ?

6. Have you ever heard of seeing with the eyes of faith?

7. If so, what do you think is meant by the expression?

THE GOOD SHEPHERD

Jesus, continuing, said: "Amen, amen I say to you: He that entereth not by the door into the sheepfold, but climbeth up another way, the same is a thief and a robber.

"But he that entereth in by the door is the shepherd of the sheep.

"To him the porter openeth; and the sheep hear his voice: and he calleth his own sheep by name, and leadeth them out.

"And when he hath let out his own sheep, he goeth before them: and the sheep follow him, because they know his voice.

[75]

"But a stranger they follow not, but fly from him, because they know not the voice of strangers.

"This proverb Jesus spoke to them. But they understood not what He spoke to them."

(In the Old Testament, the figure of the shepherd is sometimes used in a spiritual sense. Because of this fact, Our Saviour's allusion, on this occasion, ought to have had a familiar sound to His hearers, but the Pharisees could not or would not understand it.)

"Jesus therefore said to them again: Amen, amen I say to you, I am the Door of the sheep.

"All others, as many as have come, are thieves and robbers: and the sheep heard them not.

"I am the Door. By Me, if any man enter in, he shall be saved: and he shall go in, and go out, and shall find pastures.

"The thief cometh not, but for to steal, and to kill, and to destroy. I am come that they may have life, and may have it more abundantly.

"I am the Good Shepherd. The Good Shepherd giveth His life for His sheep.

"But the hireling, and he that is not the shepherd, and whose own the sheep are not, seeth the wolf coming, and leaveth the sheep, and flieth: and the wolf catcheth, and scattereth the sheep:

"And the hireling flieth, because he is a hireling: and he hath no care for the sheep.

JESUS IN JERUSALEM

"I am the Good Shepherd; and I know Mine, and Mine know Me.

"As the Father knoweth Me, and I know the Father: and I lay down My life for My sheep." (St. John x, 1–15.)

QUESTIONS

1. Read the story of the Good Shepherd.

2. What is meant in this story by a "hireling"?

3. Jesus said: "I am the Good Shepherd." In what way is Jesus a Good Shepherd?

OTHER SHEEP I HAVE

"And other sheep I have, that are not of this fold: them also I must bring, and they shall hear My voice, and there shall be one fold and one Shepherd.

"Therefore doth the Father love Me: because I lay down My life, that I may take it again.

"No man taketh it away from Me: but I lay it down of Myself, and I have power to lay it down: and I have power to take it up again. This commandment have I received of My Father."

These last words left the people divided in opinion and feeling, and many of them said: "He hath a devil, and is mad: why hear you Him?" Others, more favorably inclined to Him, mingled their voices

[77]

with those of the slanderers, and said: "These are not the words of one that hath a devil: Can a devil open the eyes of the blind?" (St. John x, 16–21.)

QUESTIONS

1. Whom do you think Jesus meant by "Other sheep I have"?

2. Tell in your own words the meaning of, "I lay down My life, that I may take it again."

3. Quote the words of this chapter which prove that Christ of His own free will laid down His life for us.

XIV

JESUS ON THE WAY FROM JERUSALEM

THE MISSION OF THE SEVENTY-TWO

We have seen that Jesus chose twelve Apostles. But now He chose seventy-two others from among His disciples. These He sent before Him into all the cities and towns of Judea and Perea while He continued on His way from Jerusalem.

Their special mission was to announce the approach of the Messias. Jesus, Himself, would later visit the people of these cities and towns, and would inflame the hearts of all who had listened with a good will to the preaching of the seventy-two. Jesus said: "The harvest indeed is great, but the laborers are few. Pray ye therefore the Lord of the harvest, that He send laborers into His harvest.

"Go: Behold I send you as lambs among wolves."

He instructed them that when they entered a house they were to say at once: "Peace be to this house." This was, and still is, the common form of greeting in the Orient.

He continued: "And if the son of peace be

"PEACE BE TO THIS HOUSE"

there, your peace shall rest upon him; but if not, it shall return to you.

"And in the same house, remain, eating and drinking such things as they have: for the laborer is worthy of his hire. Remove not from house to house.

"And into what city soever you enter, and they receive you, eat such things as are set before you.

"And heal the sick that are therein, and say to them: The Kingdom of God is come nigh unto you." (St. Luke x, 1–9.)

Reward and Punishment

The seventy-two disciples were to reward those who received them by healing their sick, by blessing them, and by promising them the Kingdom of God. On the other hand, if no fitting welcome were given the disciples as ambassadors of the Messias, and if their words were not listened to, then they were to leave the inhospitable people to the justice of God.

Sodom in the old days had been destroyed by fire for its wickedness; now, Our Lord declared that even the fate of Sodom would be less hard than that of the cities which should reject the men whom He was sending out.

THE JOURNEYS OF JESUS

Remembering also certain places which had rejected Him and His teaching, Our Lord said: "Woe to thee, Corozain, woe to thee, Bethsaida. For if in Tyre and Sidon had been wrought the mighty works that have been wrought in you, they would have done penance long ago, sitting in sackcloth and ashes.

"But it shall be more tolerable for Tyre and Sidon at the judgment, than for you.

"And thou, Capharnaum, which art exalted unto heaven, thou shalt be thrust down to hell."

To the seventy-two disciples He then said: "He that heareth you, heareth Me; and he that despiseth you, despiseth Me; and he that despiseth Me, despiseth Him that sent Me." (St. Luke x, 13–16.)

QUESTIONS

1. Why did Jesus send His seventy-two disciples before Him on the way from Jerusalem?

2. At the present day what should we call these seventy-two?

3. Was there any good reason why people should receive the seventy-two as sent from God?

4. Read what the Bible says of the cities of Corozain, Bethsaida, Tyre, Sidon, and Capharnaum.

5. Locate on the map the places named in this chapter.

JESUS ON THE WAY FROM JERUSALEM

The Return of the Seventy-Two

The seventy-two traveled in the direction of Judea and Perea, and, as the places visited were close to each other, lying along the banks of the Jordan, the disciples were absent from the Master only a short time. The Gospel does not tell us where they met Jesus, nor when they returned. It only reads:

"And the seventy-two returned with joy, saying: Lord, the devils also are subject to us in Thy Name.

"And He said to them: I saw Satan like lightning falling from heaven.

"Behold, I have given you power to tread upon serpents and scorpions, and upon all the power of the enemy: and nothing shall hurt you.

"But yet rejoice not in this, that spirits are subject unto you; but rejoice in this, that your names are written in heaven.

"In that same hour, He rejoiced in the Holy Ghost, and said: I confess to Thee, O Father, Lord of heaven and earth, because Thou hast hidden these things from the wise and prudent, and hast revealed them to little ones. Yea, Father, for so it hath seemed good in Thy sight.

"All things are delivered to Me by My Father; and no one knoweth Who the Son is, but the Father;

[83]

and Who the Father is, but the Son, and to whom the Son will reveal Him.

"And turning to His disciples, He said: Blessed are the eyes that see the things which you see.

"For I say to you, that many prophets and kings have desired to see the things that you see, and have not seen them; and to hear the things that you hear, and have not heard them." (St. Luke x, 17–24.)

QUESTIONS

1. Have you any reason to think that the mission of the seventy-two disciples was a success?

2. In what way did Jesus show His pleasure in their work?

3. Do the Gospels give many accounts of times when Jesus rejoiced? Find how many are noted.

4. What is your opinion of those who rejoice in the good works done by others? Think of the Gospel of St. Luke when you give your answer.

THE TWO GREAT COMMANDMENTS

"And behold a certain lawyer stood up, tempting Him, and saying: Master, what must I do to possess eternal life?

"But He said to him: What is written in the Law? how readest thou?

"He answering, said: *Thou shalt love the Lord thy*

JESUS ON THE WAY FROM JERUSALEM

God with thy whole heart, and with thy whole soul, and with all thy strength, and with all thy mind: and thy neighbor as thyself.

"And He said to him: Thou hast answered right: this do, and thou shalt live.

"But he willing to justify himself, said to Jesus: And who is my neighbor?" (St. Luke x, 25–29.)

This was a much-discussed question among the Jews; many of them regarded as neighbors only those of their own nation. To make them think rightly on this point Christ now gave the parable of the Good Samaritan.

QUESTIONS

1. Which are the Two Great Commandments?

2. The lawyer knew the Two Commandments. Do you think he was in the habit of observing them from his question, "And who is my neighbor"?

THE GOOD SAMARITAN

The road in the mountainous stretch of land through which Jesus and His companions had been journeying was frequently called the "Highway of Blood." Travelers on it were often attacked by robbers, who left their wounded victims to die, or to receive care from some passer-by. This condition of

2   [85]

affairs led Our Lord to relate a parable about such robbers and one of their victims to teach the lawyer that Samaritans and Gentiles, as well as Jews, were his "neighbors."

"And Jesus answering, said to him: A certain man went down from Jerusalem to Jericho, and fell among robbers, who also stripped him, and having wounded him went away, leaving him half dead.

"And it chanced, that a certain priest went down the same way: and seeing him, passed by.

"In like manner also a Levite, when he was near the place and saw him, passed by.

"But a certain Samaritan being on his journey, came near him; and seeing him, was moved with compassion.

"And going up to him, bound up his wounds, pouring in oil and wine: and setting him upon his own beast, brought him to an inn, and took care of him.

"And the next day he took out two pence, and gave to the host, and said: Take care of him; and whatsoever thou shalt spend over and above, I, at my return, will repay thee.

"Which of these three, in thy opinion, was neighbor to him that fell among the robbers?

"But he said: He that showed mercy to him. And Jesus said to him: Go, and do thou in like manner." (St. Luke x, 30–37.)

THE GOOD SAMARITAN

THE JOURNEYS OF JESUS

Some think that the story of the Good Samaritan was not a parable but a real narrative of facts; for the road mentioned in the parable passes through a secluded region—a favorite haunt for robbers. The spot is still shown where the Good Samaritan is supposed to have done his deed of charity. Near the spot is the Well of the Apostles.

QUESTIONS

1. Locate Jericho on the map.

2. Who are our neighbors?

3. Read the whole story of the Good Samaritan.

4. Find three ways in which we can resemble the Good Samaritan.

XV

JESUS AT BETHANY

MARTHA AND MARY

Jesus was on the highroad leading to Jerusalem. However, He stopped at "a certain town: and a certain woman named Martha, received Him into her house. And she had a sister called Mary."

When Jesus entered, the two sisters hastened to do Him all honor, but each in her own way. "Martha was busy about much serving," so that we are inclined to think she was the older of the two sisters and had the care of the house. Mary, "sitting also at the Lord's feet, heard His Word."

Martha, as hostess, was eager to entertain her Guest with every mark of respect. In doing this she may have been too uneasy, for she came to the Master and, seeing Mary calmly seated at His feet, said to Him: "Lord, hast Thou no care that my sister hath left me alone to serve? speak to her therefore, that she help me."

The Saviour needed the service of Martha, and He knew it was for love of Him that she labored so

JESUS AT THE HOUSE OF MARTHA AND MARY

earnestly. When He answered her request, therefore, He did not condemn her work but only reminded her of "one thing more important." In His gentle way, He said to her: "Martha, Martha, thou art careful, and art troubled about many things:

"But one thing is necessary. Mary hath chosen the best part, which shall not be taken away from her." (St. Luke x, 38–42.)

Those monks and nuns who spend a great part of their time in prayer are said to lead a contemplative life; those who spend less time in prayer and much of their time in visiting the sick and the poor, who care for the orphans and teach, are said to lead an active life.

QUESTIONS

1. Read the story of Martha and Mary as given in the New Testament and tell why Jesus said: "Mary hath chosen the best part."

2. Did Our Lord lead an active or a contemplative life?

3. In what way do those who lead a contemplative life help their neighbors?

4. Give the name of a great saint who is a model of the active missionary life.

5. Give the name of one who is a model of the contemplative life.

6. What do you think of St. Ignatius of Loyola?

7. How did St. Teresa labor for souls?

XVI

JESUS IN PEREA

THE SECOND FORM OF THE LORD'S PRAYER

After leaving Bethany Jesus crossed the Jordan and came into the land of Perea. St. Luke tells us: "And it came to pass, that as He was in a certain place praying, when He ceased, one of His disciples said to Him: Lord, teach us to pray, as John also taught his disciples.

"And He said to them: When you pray, say: Father, hallowed be Thy Name. Thy Kingdom come.

"Give us this day our daily bread.

"And forgive us our sins, for we also forgive every one that is indebted to us. And lead us not into temptation." (St. Luke xi, 1-4.)

THE PARABLE OF THE THREE LOAVES

Then Jesus taught His disciples the value of persevering prayer. He said to them: "Which of you shall have a friend, and shall go to him at midnight, and shall say to him: Friend, lend me three loaves,

JESUS IN PRAYER

"Because a friend of mine is come off his journey to me, and I have not what to set before him.

"And he from within should answer, and say: Trouble me not, the door is now shut, and my children are with me in bed; I cannot rise and give thee.

"Yet if he shall continue knocking, I say to you, although he will not rise and give him, because he is his friend; yet, because of his importunity, he will rise, and give him as many as he needeth.

"And I say to you, Ask, and it shall be given you: seek, and you shall find: knock, and it shall be opened to you.

"For every one that asketh, receiveth; and he that seeketh, findeth; and to him that knocketh, it shall be opened.

"And which of you, if he ask his father bread, will he give him a stone? or a fish, will he for a fish give him a serpent?

"Or if he shall ask an egg, will he reach him a scorpion?

"If you then, being evil, know how to give good gifts to your children, how much more will your Father from heaven give the good Spirit to them that ask Him?" (St. Luke xi, 5–13.)

If a selfish man will grant a favor to a persistent neighbor, how much more will our heavenly Father grant our persevering prayer?

JESUS IN PEREA

QUESTIONS

1. Why did Our Lord teach the Apostles how to pray?

2. How did He teach them the need of persevering prayer?

3. How many petitions has the second form of the Lord's prayer?

4. When and where did Jesus teach the Lord's prayer in the form given in St. Matthew vi, 9–13?

THE BLIND AND DUMB DEMONIAC

At the close of the instructions on prayer, "Then was offered to Him one possessed with a devil, blind and dumb: and He healed him, so that he spoke and saw.

"And all the multitudes were amazed, and said: Is not this the Son of David?

"But the Pharisees hearing it, said: This Man casteth not out devils but by Beelzebub the Prince of the devils.

"And Jesus knowing their thoughts, said to them: Every kingdom divided against itself shall be made desolate: and every city or house divided against itself shall not stand.

"And if Satan cast out Satan, he is divided against himself: how then shall his kingdom stand?

"And if I by Beelzebub cast out devils, by whom

do your children cast them out? Therefore they shall be your judges.

"But if I by the Spirit of God cast out devils, then is the Kingdom of God come upon you.

"Or how can any one enter into the house of the strong, and rifle his goods, unless he first bind the strong? and then he will rifle his house.

"He that is not with Me, is against Me: and he that gathereth not with Me, scattereth.

"Therefore I say to you: Every sin and blasphemy shall be forgiven men, but the blasphemy of the Spirit shall not be forgiven.

"And whosoever shall speak a word against the Son of Man, it shall be forgiven him: but he that shall speak against the Holy Ghost, it shall not be forgiven him, neither in this world, nor in the world to come.

"Either make the tree good and its fruit good: or make the tree evil, and its fruit evil. For by the fruit the tree is known.

"O generation of vipers, how can you speak good things, whereas you are evil? for out of the abundance of the heart the mouth speaketh.

"A good man out of a good treasure bringeth forth good things: and an evil man out of an evil treasure bringeth forth evil things.

"But I say unto you, that every idle word that men

shall speak, they shall render an account for it in the day of judgment.

"For by thy words thou shalt be justified, and by thy words thou shalt be condemned." (St. Matthew xii, 22–37.)

QUESTIONS

1. What is blasphemy?

2. How had the Pharisees committed the sin of blasphemy?

3. What did Jesus say concerning a good and a bad tree?

THE SIGN OF JONAS

Some of the Pharisees and Scribes were much dissatisfied with all that Our Lord had said and done which plainly marked Him as the promised Messias.

"Then some of the Scribes and Pharisees answered him, saying: Master we would see a sign from Thee.

"Who answering said to them: An evil and adulterous generation seeketh a sign: and a sign shall not be given it, but the sign of Jonas the prophet.

"For as Jonas was in the whale's belly three days and three nights: so shall the Son of Man be in the heart of the earth three days and three nights.

"The men of Ninive shall rise in judgment with this generation, and shall condemn it: because they did

[97]

penance at the preaching of Jonas. And behold a greater than Jonas here.

"The queen of the south shall rise in judgment with this generation, and shall condemn it: because she came from the ends of the earth to hear the wisdom of Solomon, and behold a greater than Solomon here.

"And when an unclean spirit is gone out of a man he walketh through dry places seeking rest, and findeth none.

"Then he saith: I will return into my house from whence I came out. And coming he findeth it empty, swept, and garnished.

"Then he goeth, and taketh with him seven other spirits more wicked than himself, and they enter in and dwell there: and the last state of that man is made worse than the first. So shall it be also to this wicked generation." (St. Matthew xii, 38–45.)

QUESTIONS

1. What is the greatest proof that Christ is the Son of God?

2. Read the story of Jonas, and find out how he was a sign of Christ's Resurrection. (Jonas i–iii.)

3. How were all the miracles of Jesus signs from heaven?

A WOMAN GLORIFIETH JESUS

THE JOURNEYS OF JESUS

THE MOTHER OF JESUS IS CALLED BLESSED

We have seen how many of the people found fault with Our Lord. These had been misled by the Pharisees. But there were still a great number who were filled with admiration of Him and who praised Him for His deeds of mercy.

"A certain woman from the crowd, lifting up her voice, said to Him: Blessed is the womb that bore Thee, and the paps that gave Thee suck.

"But He said: Yea rather, blessed are they who hear the word of God, and keep it." (St. Luke xi, 27–28.)

By this answer Jesus gave the Jews to understand that there is a blessedness greater than that of any earthly motherhood; that is, the blessedness of receiving the word of God and of doing His will even as Mary, His Mother, had received His word and had done His will.

QUESTIONS

1. Why do we honor Mary?

2. Why did the woman mentioned in the lesson call her "blessed"?

3. Had she ever before been called "blessed"? If so, when and by whom?

4. When and from whom do we hear the word of God?

JESUS IN PEREA

THE PHARISEE'S BANQUET

The Jews took their first meal toward the middle of the day. On this occasion, while Jesus was still speaking to the crowd, "a certain Pharisee prayed Him, that He would dine with him. And He going in, sat down to eat." (St. Luke xi, 37.)

It would seem that the Apostles were not invited, for Jesus found Himself alone in the midst of men who were vain of their learning and envious of the place which Our Lord had made for Himself in the hearts of the people by His teaching and His miracles.

Before seating themselves at table all the guests went through their customary cleansings. They saw that Jesus sat down without observing any of these ceremonies. The Pharisees neglected the duties of love of God and their neighbors, but used the mark of outward religious observance. It was this which forced the gentle Saviour to speak to them harshly. "And the Pharisee began to say, thinking within himself, why He was not washed before dinner.

"And the Lord said to him: Now you Pharisees make clean the outside of the cup and of the platter; but your inside is full of rapine and iniquity.

"Ye fools, did not He that made that which is without, make also that which is within?" (St. Luke xi, 38–40.)

THREE WOES PRONOUNCED AGAINST THE PHARISEES

Then, with more indignation than ever, Jesus uttered a three-fold curse upon the Pharisees. He said:

"But woe to you, Pharisees, because you tithe mint and rue and every herb; and pass over judgment and the charity of God. Now these things you ought to have done, and not to leave the other undone.

"Woe to you, Pharisees, because you love the uppermost seats in the synagogues, and salutations in the market-place.

"Woe to you, because you are as sepulchres that appear not, and men that walk over are not aware." (St. Luke xi, 42–44.)

These fearless words were of course far from pleasing to the Pharisees; and there were others at the table who felt that Our Lord's words applied to them too.

"And one of the lawyers answering, saith to Him: Master, in saying these things, Thou reproachest us also.

"But He said: Woe to you lawyers also, because you load men with burdens which they cannot bear, and you yourselves touch not the packs with one of your fingers.

JESUS IN PEREA

"Woe to you who build the monuments of the prophets: and your fathers killed them.

"Truly you bear witness that you consent to the doings of your fathers: for they indeed killed them, and you build their sepulchres. . . .

"Woe to you lawyers, for you have taken away the key of knowledge: you yourselves have not entered in, and those that were entering in, you have hindered." (St. Luke xi, 45–48, 52.)

QUESTIONS

1. To what did Jesus liken the Pharisees?

2. How many "woes" did He utter against them?

3. Did He fear to tell the lawyer the truth about his conduct?

4. Do you think that "the key of knowledge" could mean explaining the Law and Doctrine of Christ?

5. Find the meaning of "tithe."

XVII

JESUS DISCOURSES ON VARIOUS SUBJECTS

BEWARE OF HYPOCRISY

Later that day, when Our Lord was again in the presence of the multitude, He began to warn His disciples against the pretended piety of the Pharisees, saying: "Beware ye of the leaven of the Pharisees, which is hypocrisy."

The foolishness of this sort of affected piety Our Lord clearly showed in the following words: "For there is nothing covered, that shall not be revealed: nor hidden, that shall not be known.

"For whatsoever things you have spoken in darkness, shall be published in the light: and that which you have spoken in the ear in the chambers, shall be preached on the housetops.

"And I say to you, My friends: Be not afraid of them who kill the body, and after that have no more that they can do.

"But I will show you Whom you shall fear: fear ye Him, Who after He hath killed, hath power

to cast into hell. Yea, I say to you, fear Him."
(St. Luke xii, 1–5.)

Jesus wished the Apostles to know that they were
always in the care of His heavenly Father and that
they need not fear to preach and confess Him before
men. He said:

"Are not five sparrows sold for two farthings, and
not one of them is forgotten before God?

"Yea, the very hairs of your head are all num-
bered. Fear not therefore: you are of more value
than many sparrows.

"And I say to you, Whosoever shall confess Me
before men, him shall the Son of Man also confess
before the angels of God.

"But he that shall deny Me before men, shall be
denied before the angels of God." (St. Luke xii,
6–9.)

QUESTIONS

1. What is hypocrisy?

2. Whom should we fear more, him who kills the body
or him who leads us into serious sins?

3. Why does Jesus here speak of sparrows?

4. How can we deny Christ before men?

BEWARE OF COVETOUSNESS

The people were listening with attention to the words of Jesus when one of the multitude, thinking of his own affairs, said to Him: "Master, speak to my brother that he divide the inheritance with me."

Jesus was speaking of heavenly things and this person was wholly concerned with a purely selfish thought. Jesus said to him: "Man, who hath appointed Me judge, or divider, over you? . . . Take heed, and beware of all covetousness; for a man's life does not consist in the abundance of things which he possesseth."

To make this truth more plain to the people, Our Lord taught them by means of a parable in these words: "The land of a certain rich man brought forth plenty of fruits.

"And he thought within himself, saying: What shall I do, because I have no room where to bestow my fruits?

"And he said: This will I do: I will pull down my barns, and will build greater; and into them will I gather all things that are grown to me, and my goods.

"And I will say to my soul: Soul, thou hast much goods laid up for many years, take thy rest; eat, drink, make good cheer.

JESUS DISCOURSES ON VARIOUS SUBJECTS

"But God said to him: Thou fool, this night do they require thy soul of thee: and whose shall those things be which thou hast provided?

"So is he that layeth up treasure for himself, and is not rich towards God." (St. Luke xii, 13–21.)

Beware of Worldly Care

Jesus continued His instructions and gave to these Perean people the very same lessons He had formerly given to the Galileans; but, now that the time of His death was fast approaching, He seemed to make His counsels even more impressive.

"And He said to His disciples: Therefore I say to you, be not solicitous for your life, what you shall eat; nor for your body, what you shall put on.

"The life is more than the meat, and the body is more than the raiment.

"Consider the ravens, for they sow not, neither do they reap, neither have they storehouse nor barn, and God feedeth them. How much are you more valuable than they?

"And which of you, by taking thought, can add to his stature one cubit?

"If then ye be not able to do so much as the least thing, why are you solicitous for the rest?

"Consider the lilies, how they grow: they labor

THE JOURNEYS OF JESUS

not, neither do they spin. But I say to you, not even Solomon in all his glory was clothed like one of these.

"Now if God clothe in this manner the grass that is to day in the field, and to morrow is cast into the oven; how much more you, O ye of little faith?

"And seek not you what you shall eat, or what you shall drink: and be not lifted up on high.

"For all these things do the nations of the world seek. But your Father knoweth that you have need of these things." (St. Luke xii, 22–30.)

QUESTIONS

1. Is it not proper for people to look ahead and plan for the future? What is the meaning of Christ's words: "Be not solicitous for your life," etc.?

2. In what way does Jesus refer to ravens, lilies, and the grass?

3. What is here meant by the words: "O ye of little faith"?

FEAR NOT, LITTLE FLOCK

Further on in this discourse, Our Lord bade the disciples not to be too careful about the things of this life, "but seek ye first the Kingdom of God and His justice, and all these things shall be added unto you." Then, speaking lovingly to those who were specially chosen to carry forward His work, He said:

JESUS DISCOURSES ON VARIOUS SUBJECTS

"Fear not, little flock, for it hath pleased your Father to give you a Kingdom.

"Sell what you possess and give alms. Make to yourselves bags which grow not old, a treasure in heaven which faileth not: where no thief approacheth, nor moth corrupteth.

"For where your treasure is, there will your heart be also." (St. Luke xii, 31–34.)

QUESTION

Can you give a meaning for the statement: "For where your treasure is, there will your heart be also"?

THE WATCHFUL SERVANT

The Orientals wore long flowing garments which, unless fastened up or girdled, prevented them from walking about with ease. Thinking of this familiar manner of dress, the Saviour took occasion to say to the Apostles: "Let your loins be girt, and lamps burning in your hands.

"And you yourselves like to men who wait for their lord, when he shall return from the wedding; that when he cometh and knocketh, they may open to him immediately." (St. Luke xii, 35–36.)

It was a Jewish custom to hold wedding-feasts at night. The time of closing the feast was uncertain; so, too, was the time of the master's return to his home. He might come at the second or the third watch; that is, at nine P.M. or at three A.M.

The Saviour continued: "Blessed are those servants, whom the Lord when He cometh, shall find watching. Amen I say to you, that He will gird Himself, and make them sit down to meat, and passing will minister unto them.

"And if He shall come in the second watch, or come in the third watch, and find them so, blessed are those servants.

"But this know ye, that if the householder did know at what hour the thief would come, he would surely watch, and would not suffer his house to be broken open.

"Be you then also ready: for at what hour you think not, the Son of Man will come."

Peter thought that the reward was intended only for the Apostles, and he said to Jesus: "Lord, dost Thou speak this parable to us, or likewise to all?

"And the Lord said: Who (thinkest thou) is the faithful and wise steward, whom his lord setteth over his family, to give them their measure of wheat in due season?

"Blessed is that servant, whom when his lord shall come, he shall find so doing.

"Verily I say to you, he will set him over all that he possesseth.

JESUS DISCOURSES ON VARIOUS SUBJECTS

"But if that servant shall say in his heart: My lord is long a coming; and shall begin to strike the menservants and maidservants, and to eat and to drink and be drunk:

"The lord of that servant will come in the day that he hopeth not, and at the hour that he knoweth not, and shall separate him, and shall appoint him his portion with unbelievers.

"And that servant who knew the will of his lord, and prepared not himself, and did not according to his will, shall be beaten with many stripes.

"But he that knew not, and did things worthy of stripes, shall be beaten with few stripes. And unto whomsoever much is given, of him much shall be required: and to whom they have committed much, of him they will demand the more." (St. Luke xii, 37–48.)

QUESTIONS

1. Is death a punishment for sin?

2. Are sickness and death always a punishment for actual sins?

3. What do you think is the best preparation that can be made for death?

4. What do you think is the meaning of these words: "Blessed are those servants, whom the Lord when He cometh, shall find watching"?

[111]

THE JOURNEYS OF JESUS

The Galileans Slain

While Jesus was still in Perea, a rumor came to Him of some men from Galilee who had attempted to throw off the yoke of Rome. Pilate's soldiers had attacked and killed them in front of the great altar where they were offering a sacrifice to God. Their blood and the blood of the victims on the altar had mingled.

The Jews at once came to the conclusion that these Galilean men had committed some awful crime for which God now permitted their terrible death. Some of the Jews hastened to where Jesus was and gave Him a full account of the massacre. Jesus knew their thoughts. He said to them: "Think you that these Galileans were sinners above all the men of Galilee, because they suffered such things?

"No, I say to you: but unless you shall do penance, you shall all likewise perish.

"Or those eighteen upon whom the tower fell in Siloe, and slew them: think you, that they also were debtors above all the men that dwelt in Jerusalem?

"No, I say to you; but except you do penance, you shall all likewise perish." (St. Luke xiii, 2–5.)

JESUS DISCOURSES ON VARIOUS SUBJECTS

The Barren Fig Tree

To teach His disciples that all the sufferings and trials of life are not sent as chastisements for actual sins, and to impress upon them the necessity of good works, Jesus related the parable of the fig tree. Figs and grapes are among the most common products of Palestine. The fig tree requires much ploughing and digging to make it produce fruit; it usually bears fruit the third year after being planted.

"A certain man had a fig tree planted in his vineyard, and he came seeking fruit on it, and found none.

"And he said to the dresser of the vineyard: Behold, for these three years I come seeking fruit on this fig tree, and I find none. Cut it down therefore: why cumbereth it the ground?

"But he answering, said to him: Lord, let it alone this year also, until I dig about it, and dung it.

"And if happily it bear fruit: but if not, then after that thou shalt cut it down." (St. Luke xiii, 6–9.)

The people of Israel had often been compared to the fig tree and its fruit. The multitudes might, therefore, have easily understood that the tree and its fruit represented the Israelites; the owner of the vineyard was the Heavenly Father; and Jesus, Himself, was the dresser or tiller who had spent almost three years

[113]

in preaching His divine doctrines and caring for the people by His miracles.

After so much tender care and constant labor, the Heavenly Father had the right to expect the fruits of penance and good works from the people, especially those of Judea and Jerusalem. But He found that the hearts of many were far from Him.

QUESTIONS

1. Try to explain to the class how "The Barren Fig Tree" represents some people of our present time.

2. About how long a time did the Public Ministry of Jesus last?

3. In what way did the people of that period resemble a barren fig tree?

The Healing of the Crippled Woman

The common people, with the exception of those whose minds had been turned against Our Lord by the Pharisees who disliked His life and teachings, seem to have welcomed Him everywhere. So here in Perea the simple-hearted people were ready to hear His words. This is shown by the fact that He spoke in their synagogue on the Sabbath.

"And behold there was a woman, who had a spirit of infirmity eighteen years: and she was bowed together, neither could she look upwards at all."

[114]

CHRIST HEALETH THE INFIRM WOMAN

Touched by her great misery, Jesus "called her
unto Him, and said to her: Woman, thou art delivered from thy infirmity.

"And He laid His hands upon her, and immediately she was made straight, and glorified God."

We may be sure that the common people were glad
of this wonderful cure, but not so the ruler of the
synagogue. The Gospel tells us that he was angry
because Jesus healed on the Sabbath. He said to the
people:

"Six days there are wherein you ought to work. In
them therefore come, and be healed; and not on the
Sabbath day."

Jesus answered not him alone, but all His enemies
there present, whose evil feelings towards Himself,
He knew well. He said: "Ye hypocrites, doth not
every one of you, on the Sabbath day, loose his
ox or his ass from the manger, and lead them to
water?

"And ought not this daughter of Abraham, whom
Satan hath bound, lo, these eighteen years, be loosed
from this bond on the Sabbath day?"

This reply made His enemies ashamed of themselves, and it pleased the common people very
much. St. Luke tells us that they "rejoiced for all
the things that were gloriously done by Him."
(St. Luke xiii, 11–17.)

JESUS DISCOURSES ON VARIOUS SUBJECTS

THE MUSTARD SEED AND THE LEAVEN

As Jesus went through the cities and towns of Perea He repeated the parables of the mustard seed and the leaven, which He had formerly uttered for the people of Galilee. No doubt He wished to make His hearers understand that in spite of all opposition the Kingdom of God, represented by the tiny mustard seed, would triumph in the end.

"He said therefore: To what is the Kingdom of God like, and whereunto shall I resemble it?

"It is like to a grain of mustard seed, which a man took and cast into his garden, and it grew and became a great tree, and the birds of the air lodged in the branches thereof."

The parable of the leaven has almost the same meaning as that of the mustard seed, except that it refers more especially to the internal growth of the Church. As the leaven works quietly and slowly in the dough, so the Church has grown slowly but constantly through the power of the Holy Ghost Who dwells within her.

"And again he said: Whereunto shall I esteem the Kingdom of God to be like?

"It is like to leaven, which a woman took and hid in three measures of meal till the whole was leavened." (St. Luke xiii, 18–21.)

THE JOURNEYS OF JESUS

QUESTIONS

1. In what way does the mustard seed remind you of the Church?

2. How does the leaven resemble the action of grace in the soul?

3. Read the parables of the mustard seed and the leaven.

AN EIGHTH JOURNEY
OF JESUS

During this journey Jesus traveled through Judea to Jerusalem, thence back across the Jordan. While He was traveling through the towns and cities of Perea, Our Saviour heard of the death of Lazarus, and returned to Bethany. After the resurrection of Lazarus, He went into a hilly country near a city called Ephrem, which is about sixteen miles northeast of Jerusalem.

The principal things to be remembered about this journey are:

The Narrow Way to Heaven
The Attempt of the Pharisees to Frighten Jesus
The Lament over the Holy City
The Pharisee's Banquet
The Healing of the Dropsy
The Parable about Manners
The Parable of the Great Supper
The Cost of Being a Disciple of Jesus
The Three Parables of Mercy
The Parable of the Unjust Steward
The Parable of the Rich Man and Lazarus
The Illness and Death of Lazarus

THE JOURNEYS OF JESUS

Lazarus Called back to Life
The Meeting at the Hill of Evil Council
The Prophecy of Caiphas
The Decree of Jesus' Death
The Retirement to Ephrem

XVIII

JESUS BEYOND THE JORDAN

The Narrow Gate

After Jesus reached Bethabara or Bethania across the Jordan, many people came to Him because their hearts had been prepared to receive His Gospel by the preaching of John the Baptist.

A certain man among them said to Jesus: "Lord, are they few that are saved?"

The Master knew well the self-confidence of these men and did not answer this question directly, but said: "Strive to enter by the narrow gate; for many, I say to you, shall seek to enter, and shall not be able.

"But when the Master of the house shall be gone in, and shall shut the door, you shall begin to stand without, and knock at the door, saying: Lord, open to us. And He answering, shall say to you: I know you not, whence you are.

"Then you shall begin to say: We have eaten and drunk in Thy presence, and Thou hast taught in our streets.

"And He shall say to you: I know you not, whence you are: depart from Me, all ye workers of iniquity.

"There shall be weeping and gnashing of teeth, when you shall see Abraham and Isaac and Jacob, and all the prophets, in the Kingdom of God, and you yourselves thrust out.

"And there shall come from the east and the west, and the north and the south; and shall sit down in the Kingdom of God.

"And behold, they are last that shall be first; and they are first that shall be last." (St. Luke xiii, 23–30.)

THE PHARISEES ATTEMPT TO FRIGHTEN JESUS

It was generally known that Jesus intended to go up to Jerusalem for the Feast of Dedication, but the Pharisees of Perea were impatient at His slow departure, and so urged Him to leave the country, saying to Him: "Depart, and get Thee hence, for Herod hath a mind to kill Thee."

Herod may have feared the censure of the Divine Preacher and made threats against Him, as he had seized and imprisoned John the Baptist; yet it was the Pharisees themselves who were desirous of having Jesus in Judea, where they felt freer to act.

But their threatening words had no effect on the

Saviour. Nothing would hinder Him from fulfilling His mission, even to the end. He would soon leave that country, not because of Herod's threats, but from obedience to the command of His heavenly Father, directing Him toward Jerusalem.

Turning to the Pharisees, Jesus said: "Go and tell that fox, Behold, I cast out devils, and do cures to day and to morrow, and the third day I am consummated.

"Nevertheless I must walk to day and to morrow, and the day following, because it cannot be that a prophet perish, out of Jerusalem."

And so at the time fixed by Himself, the Saviour quitted Perea, crossed over the Jordan, and took the road that led to the Holy City. As He was nearing the walls of the city, His tender heart became sad. Knowing the things that would come to pass, He mourned for its people and said: "Jerusalem, Jerusalem, that killest the prophets, and stonest them that are sent to thee, how often would I have gathered thy children as the bird doth her brood under her wings, and thou wouldest not?

"Behold your house shall be left to you desolate. And I say to you, that you shall not see Me till the time come, when you shall say: Blessed is He that cometh in the Name of the Lord." (St. Luke xiii, 31-35.)

THE JOURNEYS OF JESUS

QUESTIONS

1. Why were the Pharisees of Perea anxious to have Jesus leave their country?

2. Why did Herod fear Jesus?

3. Why did Jesus call him "that fox"?

4. What reasons led Jesus to leave the Perean country?

5. Locate the places mentioned in the last two chapters.

XIX

JESUS IN JERUSALEM

THE FEAST OF DEDICATION

"And it was the Feast of the Dedication at Jerusalem: and it was winter.

"And Jesus walked in the Temple, in Solomon's porch."

The feast, the season, and the place are mentioned by the Evangelist, St. John.

The feast was celebrated with great solemnity in the month of December and continued for eight days. A special feature of the celebration was the kindling of the lights in the houses, to commemorate the new fire lit in the Temple. Hence this feast was also called the "Feast of Lights."

The feast was instituted by Judas Machabeus to arouse in the people sentiments of gratitude towards God for their deliverance from the idol-worship introduced into the Temple by Antiochus.

The scene of the festivity was in that part of the Temple which was known as Solomon's porch; we should call it a colonnade or veranda. Through this colonnade Our Saviour walked up and down while He taught the people.

The Jewish leaders of the people took this opportunity when Jesus was not surrounded by so great a multitude to gather round about Him and say to Him:

"How long dost Thou hold our souls in suspense? If Thou be the Christ, tell us plainly.

"Jesus answered them: I speak to you, and you believe not: the works that I do in the Name of My Father, they give testimony of Me.

"But you do not believe, because you are not of My sheep.

"My sheep hear My voice: and I know them, and they follow Me.

"And I give them life everlasting; and they shall not perish for ever, and no man shall pluck them out of My hand.

"That which My Father hath given Me, is greater than all: and no one can snatch them out of the hand of My Father.

"I and the Father are One."

Jesus thus declared Himself their God, and answered their question: "If Thou be the Christ, tell us plainly." For this very answer, "the Jews then took up stones to stone Him."

With mild words Jesus replied to this madness.

He said to them: "Many good works I have showed you from My Father; for which of those works do you stone Me?

"The Jews answered Him: For a good work we stone Thee not, but for blasphemy; and because that Thou, being a man, makest Thyself God." (St. John x, 22–33.)

The Jews now attempted to take Him, intending either to stone Him or to make Him a prisoner. But "He escaped out of their hands," probably in a miraculous way. Then Jesus went out of the Temple, and returned to the other side of the Jordan, where a kindly welcome was given to Him.

He visited again the places where John had baptized; the people gathered round Him and said: "John indeed did no sign.

"But all things whatsoever John said of this Man, were true. And many believed in Him." (St. John x, 39–42.)

XX

JESUS IN THE HOUSE OF THE PHARISEE

He Heals a Man who Had Dropsy

It was about this time that Our Lord performed another of His miracles of compassion, by healing a man who had dropsy. This He did in the house of a Pharisee, where He had been invited to dine, on a Sabbath day. It is difficult to determine whether He had been invited through kindness or through some evil intention of watching Him for the purpose of finding fault with Him. The Gospel does not tell us about this, nor does it explain the presence of the sick man.

Looking upon this man, Jesus read the thoughts of the guests and, as if answering them, spoke "to the lawyers and Pharisees, saying: Is it lawful to heal on the Sabbath day?"

The Pharisees looked at one another, "but they held their peace." No one replied. If they had said "It is lawful," they would have been neglecting their traditions; if they had said "It is not lawful," they would have been blamed by the multitude. Their

JESUS IN THE HOUSE OF THE PHARISEE

silence left Jesus free to act. "But He taking him, healed him, and sent him away."

Then, turning toward the Pharisees, Jesus said: "Which of you shall have an ass or an ox fall into a pit, and will not immediately draw him out, on the Sabbath day?" And they could not answer, but began to take their places at the table. (St. Luke xiv, 1–6.)

QUESTIONS

1. Why did not the Pharisees answer the question Jesus addressed to them?

2. Is it ever lawful to work on Sunday?

3. Name some works that are considered servile works.

4. Can you give a good reason for doing servile works on Sunday?

5. When we give alms, or help the sick and poor, what should be our motive?

A Lesson in Manners and Charity

"And He spoke a parable also to them that were invited, marking how they chose the first seats at the table, saying to them:

"When thou art invited to a wedding, sit not down in the first place, lest perhaps one more honorable than thou be invited by him:

"And he that invited thee and him, come and say to thee, Give this man place: and then thou begin with shame to take the lowest place.

"But when thou art invited, go, sit down in the lowest place; that when he who invited thee, cometh, he may say to thee: Friend, go up higher. Then shalt thou have glory before them that sit at table with thee.

"Because every one that exalteth himself, shall be humbled; and he that humbleth himself, shall be exalted.

"And He said to him also that had invited Him: When thou makest a dinner or a supper, call not thy friends, nor thy brethren, nor thy kinsmen, nor thy neighbors who are rich; lest perhaps they also invite thee again, and a recompense be made to thee.

"But when thou makest a feast, call the poor, the maimed, the lame, and the blind;

"And thou shalt be blessed, because they have not wherewith to make thee recompense: for recompense shall be made thee at the resurrection of the just." (St. Luke xiv, 7–14.)

QUESTIONS

1. Can you name a lesson taught by Jesus at the banquet of the Pharisee?

2. Why should we place ourselves below others?

JESUS IN THE HOUSE OF THE PHARISEE

The Parable of the Great Supper

We may be sure that such direct words as these were distasteful to the Scribes. It was unbearable to them to think that the miserable people for whom the Saviour had just pleaded would ever be placed on an equal footing with them, or have power to bestow eternal favors upon them. So one of those who sat at table with Jesus, said in a boasting manner: "Blessed is he that shall eat bread in the Kingdom of God."

And Jesus replied by relating this parable: "A certain man made a great supper, and invited many.

"And he sent his servant at the hour of supper to say to them that were invited, that they should come, for now all things are ready.

"And they began all at once to make excuse. The first said to him: I have bought a farm, and I must needs go out and see it: I pray thee, hold me excused.

"And another said: I have bought five yoke of oxen, and I go to try them: I pray thee, hold me excused.

"And another said: I have married a wife, and therefore I cannot come.

"And the servant returning, told these things to

his lord. Then the master of the house, being angry, said to his servant: Go out quickly into the streets and lanes of the city, and bring in hither the poor, and the feeble, and the blind, and the lame.

"And the servant said: Lord, it is done as thou hast commanded, and yet there is room.

"And the Lord said to the servant: Go out into the highways and hedges, and compel them to come in, that my house may be filled.

"But I say unto you, that none of those men that were invited, shall taste of my supper." (St. Luke xiv, 15–24.)

In this story lies the great truth that nothing can excuse those who deliberately refuse the call to the Kingdom of Heaven; and that those who, having received the invitation, set it aside for pleasure, or gain, or earthly affection, will be excluded forever from the delights that are prepared for those who love and serve God.

QUESTIONS

1. Is there any duty which can prevent us from serving God?

2. How can we make our good works pleasing to God?

3. Give in your own words the meaning of this sentence: "None of these men that were invited, shall taste of my supper."

JESUS IN THE HOUSE OF THE PHARISEE

Counting the Cost of Being a Disciple of Jesus

The Saviour gave three illustrations to show the necessity of counting beforehand the cost of being His disciple.

"For which of you having a mind to build a tower, doth not first sit down, and reckon the charges that are necessary, whether he have wherewithal to finish it:

"Lest, after he hath laid the foundation, and is not able to finish it, all that see it begin to mock him,

"Saying: This man began to build, and was not able to finish.

"Or what king, about to go to make war against another king, doth not first sit down, and think whether he be able, with ten thousand, to meet him that, with twenty thousand, cometh against him?

"Or else, whilst the other is yet afar off, sending an embassy, he desireth conditions of peace.

"So likewise every one of you that doth not renounce all that he possesseth, cannot be My disciple.

"Salt is good. But if the salt shall lose its savor, wherewith shall it be seasoned?

"It is neither profitable for the land nor for the dunghill, but shall be cast out. He that hath ears to hear, let him hear." (St. Luke xiv, 28–35.)

THE JOURNEYS OF JESUS

QUESTIONS

1. Why did Christ so often utter these last words at the close of His instructions?

2. What earthly possessions did the Apostles leave to follow Jesus?

3. Who renounce for God's sake all that they possess?

4. Can you remember the reward promised by God to those who give up all for His sake? If so, what is it?

5. What do the dead take with them into the next life?

XXI

THREE PARABLES OF MERCY

THE LOST SHEEP

About this time Jesus related a series of parables to show the tender mercy of the Heavenly Father for His weak, sinful, and straying children.

In these three parables of the Lost Sheep, the Lost Groat, and the Prodigal Son, the loving care of the Father for the welfare of each immortal soul is clearly stated. It was no wonder that "publicans and sinners drew near unto Him to hear Him.

"And the Pharisees and Scribes murmured, saying: This Man receiveth sinners, and eateth with them."

Jesus replied to the grumbling Pharisees with the parable of the Lost Sheep. He said:

"What man of you that hath an hundred sheep: and if he shall lose one of them, doth he not leave the ninety-nine in the desert, and go after that which was lost, until he find it?

"And when he hath found it, lay it upon his shoulders, rejoicing:

THE GOOD SHEPHERD

THREE PARABLES OF MERCY

"And coming home, call together his friends and neighbors, saying to them: Rejoice with me, because I have found my sheep that was lost?

"I say to you, that even so there shall be joy in heaven upon one sinner that doth penance, more than upon ninety-nine just who need not penance." (St. Luke xv, 1–7.)

QUESTION

Can you give any reason for Christ's relating so many parables about sheep and shepherds?

THE LOST GROAT

In the East, women wear pieces of money as ornaments upon their heads. At birth they receive their first piece, and all pieces, the gold of the rich and the silver of the poor, are gifts which they have received upon various occasions. The coins are never spent but are kept in the family, and, as heirlooms, are handed down from mother to daughter. Since the coins are prized above all value, the throng listening to Our Saviour understood this parable of the Lost Groat:

"Or what woman having ten groats; if she lose one groat, doth not light a candle, and sweep the house, and seek diligently until she find it?

[137]

"And when she hath found it, call together her friends and neighbors, saying: Rejoice with me, because I have found the groat which I had lost.

"So I say to you, there shall be joy before the angels of God upon one sinner doing penance." (St. Luke xv, 8–10.)

THE PRODIGAL SON

Most impressive of the parables was this of the Prodigal Son, which shows the loving forgiveness of a father for the misconduct of a spendthrift son.

"A certain man had two sons:

"And the younger of them said to his father: Father, give me the portion of substance that falleth to me. And he divided unto them his substance.

"And not many days after, the younger son, gathering all together, went abroad into a far country: and there wasted his substance, living riotously.

"And after he had spent all, there came a mighty famine in that country; and he began to be in want.

"And he went and cleaved to one of the citizens of that country. And he sent him into his farm to feed swine.

"And he would fain have filled his belly with the husks the swine did eat; and no man gave unto him.

"And returning to himself, he said: How many

THE DEPARTURE OF THE PRODIGAL SON

hired servants in my father's house abound with bread, and I here perish with hunger?

"I will arise, and will go to my father, and say to him: Father, I have sinned against heaven, and before thee:

"I am not worthy to be called thy son: make me as one of thy hired servants.

"And rising up he came to his father. And when he was yet a great way off, his father saw him, and was moved with compassion, and running to him fell upon his neck, and kissed him.

"And the son said to him: Father, I have sinned against heaven, and before thee, I am not now worthy to be called thy son.

"And the father said to his servants: Bring forth quickly the first robe, and put it on him, and put a ring on his hand, and shoes on his feet:

"And bring hither the fatted calf, and kill it, and let us eat and make merry:

"Because this my son was dead, and is come to life again: was lost, and is found. And they began to be merry.

"Now his elder son was in the field, and when he came and drew nigh to the house, he heard music and dancing:

"And he called one of the servants, and asked what these things meant.

THE RETURN OF THE PRODIGAL SON

"And he said to him: Thy brother is come, and thy father hath killed the fatted calf, because he hath received him safe.

"And he was angry, and would not go in. His father therefore coming out began to entreat him.

"And he answering, said to his father: Behold, for so many years do I serve thee, and I have never transgressed thy commandment, and yet thou hast never given me a kid to make merry with my friends:

"But as soon as this thy son is come, who hath devoured his substance with harlots, thou hast killed for him the fatted calf.

"But he said to him: Son, thou art always with me, and all I have is thine.

"But it was fit that we should make merry and be glad, for this thy brother was dead and is come to life again; he was lost, and is found." (St. Luke xv, 11–32.)

QUESTIONS

1. Tell in your own words the story of the Prodigal Son.

2. What events caused the prodigal to think of his father and home?

3. In what sense was this son "dead"?

4. Had the son who remained at home any reason to complain of his father's conduct towards the repentant son?

XXII

JESUS IN THE LAND BEYOND THE JORDAN

THE UNJUST STEWARD

Another parable was spoken by Our Lord at this time to show how those possessed of great worldly goods might use them wisely to obtain eternal life.

"And He said also to His disciples: There was a certain rich man who had a steward: and the same was accused unto him, that he had wasted his goods.

"And he called him, and said to him: How is it that I hear this of thee? give an account of thy stewardship: for now thou canst be steward no longer.

"And the steward said within himself: What shall I do, because my lord taketh away from me the stewardship? To dig I am not able; to beg I am ashamed.

"I know what I will do, that when I shall be removed from the stewardship, they may receive me into their houses.

"Therefore calling together every one of his lord's debtors, he said to the first: How much dost thou owe my lord?

"But he said: An hundred barrels of oil. And he said to him: Take thy bill and sit down quickly, and write fifty.

"Then he said to another: And how much dost thou owe? Who said: An hundred quarters of wheat. He said to him: Take thy bill, and write eighty.

"And the lord commended the unjust steward, forasmuch as he had done wisely: for the children of this world are wiser in their generation than the children of light.

"And I say to you: Make unto you friends of the mammon of iniquity; that when you shall fail, they may receive you into everlasting dwellings.

"He that is faithful in that which is least, is faithful also in that which is greater: and he that is unjust in that which is little, is unjust also in that which is greater.

"If then you have not been faithful in the unjust mammon; who will trust you with that which is the true?

"And if you have not been faithful in that which is another's; who will give you that which is your own?

"No servant can serve two masters: for either he will hate the one, and love the other; or he will hold to the one, and despise the other. You cannot serve God and mammon.

"Now the Pharisees, who were covetous, heard all these things: and they derided Him.

"And He said to them: You are they who justify yourselves before men, but God knoweth your hearts; for that which is high to men, is an abomination before God." (St. Luke xvi, 1–15.)

QUESTIONS

1. How did the steward try to make friends for himself after the rich man accused him of wasting his goods?

2. Can you tell in what way he acted wisely?

3. Who are meant by "the children of this world"?

4. Who are "the children of light"?

5. What is here said of those who are faithful in little deeds?

6. What does it mean to covet what belongs to others?

7. What can you say of those who can justify their evil works before men?

8. Who alone can see the intention of our actions?

THE RICH MAN AND LAZARUS

Again the Saviour spoke of riches, and the dangers that beset those who are in possession of earthly goods. The subject was a disagreeable one to the Pharisees, who were rich and loved riches. But Our Lord did not hesitate to rebuke those who put their trust entirely in wealth. He said: "There was a certain rich man, who was clothed in purple and fine linen; and feasted sumptuously every day.

"And there was a certain beggar, named Lazarus, who lay at his gate, full of sores,

"Desiring to be filled with crumbs that fell from the rich man's table, and no one did give him; moreover the dogs came, and licked his sores.

"And it came to pass, that the beggar died, and was carried by the angels into Abraham's bosom. And the rich man also died: and he was buried in hell.

"And lifting up his eyes when he was in torments, he saw Abraham afar off, and Lazarus in his bosom:

"And he cried, and said: Father Abraham, have mercy on me, and send Lazarus, that he may dip the tip of his finger in water, to cool my tongue: for I am tormented in this flame.

"And Abraham said to him: Son, remember that thou didst receive good things in thy lifetime, and likewise Lazarus evil things, but now he is comforted; and thou art tormented.

"And besides all this, between us and you, there is fixed a great chaos: so that they who would pass from hence to you, cannot, nor from thence come hither.

"And he said: Then, father, I beseech thee, that

LAZARUS AND THE RICH MAN

thou wouldst send him to my father's house, for I have five brethren,

"That he may testify unto them, lest they also come into this place of torments.

"And Abraham said to him: They have Moses and the prophets; let them hear them.

"But he said: No, father Abraham: but if one went to them from the dead, they will do penance.

"And he said to him: If they hear not Moses and the prophets, neither will they believe, if one rise again from the dead." (St. Luke xvi, 19–31.)

QUESTIONS

1. From Whom do all riches come?

2. Show how they may become a blessing to their possessor.

3. From the parable of "The Rich Man and Lazarus" show how riches may be abused.

4. What message did the rich man wish to send to his five brethren?

5. What answer did Abraham give to this request?

6. Do you think people who lead evil lives would change their conduct if a messenger from the dead should come to them?

XXIII

JESUS IN THE LAND OF PEREA

The Sickness of Lazarus

Bethania, or Bethany, was a village about two miles southeast of Jerusalem. Here dwelt a family consisting of the two sisters, Martha and Mary, of whom we have read before, and a brother, Lazarus. They were friends of Jesus, and they had entertained Him in their home; so when Lazarus about this time fell sick and seemed near death, his sisters sent a messenger to Our Lord, saying: "Lord, behold, he whom Thou lovest is sick."

But Jesus hearing this only said: "This sickness is not unto death, but for the glory of God: that the Son of God may be glorified by it.

"Now Jesus loved Martha, and her sister Mary, and Lazarus.

"When He had heard therefore that he was sick, He still remained in the same place two days." (St. John xi, 3–6.)

This was not because He was indifferent to the sorrows of the family, for He loved them; but because

2   [149]

His mission required Him to stay longer in Perea, and also because He wished to make more striking the miracle which He intended to perform.

The Death of Lazarus

At Bethania what eager expectation, what anxious watching of the road from the mountains of Perea to the footpath that led to the town! Alas, for their useless and forlorn hopes! Lazarus died on the same day that the messengers reached Jesus; and, as is the custom in warm climates, his body was wrapped at once in perfumes and linen bands, and was carried to the grave amidst the wailing of the mourners.

Jesus had not spoken of Bethania or of Lazarus during the two days of waiting; on the third day He said to His disciples: "Let us go into Judea again."

The disciples said to Him: "Rabbi, the Jews but now sought to stone Thee: and goest Thou thither again?

"Jesus answered: Are there not twelve hours of the day? If a man walk in the day, he stumbleth not, because he seeth the light of this world:

"But if he walk in the night, he stumbleth, because the light is not in him."

He made no reference to the Jews or to their treatment of Him, but went on to say: "Lazarus our friend sleepeth; but I go that I may awake him out of sleep."

The disciples forgot that the daughter of Jairus had been awakened by the Master from the sleep of death,[1] and, as ever slow to understand His meaning, they responded: "Lord, if he sleep, he shall do well.

"But Jesus spoke of his death; and they thought that He spoke of the repose of sleep.

"Then therefore Jesus said to them plainly: Lazarus is dead.

"And I am glad, for your sakes, that I was not there, that you may believe: but let us go to him."

Fear of returning to Judea was still strong in the hearts of the Apostles. They did not relish going again among those who had proved their enmity to Christ so plainly. They felt that His followers would share in the hatred sure to be shown to their Master. They seem to have hesitated when Our Lord proposed to go to Lazarus, for we are told that St. Thomas, who was called Didymus, turned to his fellow disciples and said: "Let us also go, that we may die with Him." (St. John xi, 7–16.)

[1] See "Journeys of Jesus, Book One," pp. 160–162.

THE JOURNEYS OF JESUS

QUESTIONS

1. Why did Our Lord say "I am glad, for your sakes, that I was not there"?

2. In what way did the Apostle Thomas show his loving devotion to Christ?

XXIV

JESUS IN BETHANIA

THE RESURRECTION OF LAZARUS

Starting in the direction of Bethania, Jesus crossed the Jordan and reached the outskirts of the village. By this time Lazarus had been four days in the tomb, but many friends of the family still lingered with Martha and Mary to comfort them.

Martha, when she heard of the arrival of Jesus, went out to meet Him and said to Him: "Lord, if Thou hadst been here, my brother had not died.

"But now also I know that whatsoever Thou wilt ask of God, God will give it Thee.

"Jesus saith to her: Thy brother shall rise again.

"Martha saith to Him: I know that he shall rise again, in the resurrection at the last day."

Martha little understood the meaning of the Saviour's promise, and thought that His words were only words of consolation. But Jesus expressed to her His true meaning when He said: "I am the Resurrection and the Life: he that believeth in Me, although he be dead, shall live:

"And every one that liveth, and believeth in Me, shall not die for ever. Believest thou this?

"She saith to Him: Yea, Lord, I have believed that Thou art Christ the Son of the living God, Who art come into this world."

Then, feeling that Mary would better understand the words of Jesus, Martha went and called her sister, Mary. Martha said to her secretly: "The Master is come, and calleth for thee.

"She, as soon as she heard this, riseth quickly, and cometh to Him. . . .

"The Jews therefore, who were with her in the house, and comforted her, when they saw Mary that she rose up speedily and went out, followed her, saying: She goeth to the grave to weep there.

"When Mary therefore was come where Jesus was, seeing Him, she fell down at His feet, and saith to Him: Lord, if Thou hadst been here, my brother had not died." She could say no more.

"Jesus, therefore, when He saw her weeping, and the Jews that were come with her, weeping, groaned in the spirit, and troubled Himself,

"And said: Where have you laid him? They say to Him: Lord, come and see.

"And Jesus wept.

"The Jews therefore said: Behold how He loved him.

"LAZARUS, COME FORTH!"

"But some of them said: Could not He that opened the eyes of the man born blind, have caused that this man should not die?

"Jesus therefore again groaning in Himself, cometh to the sepulchre. Now it was a cave; and a stone was laid over it.

"Jesus saith: Take away the stone."

At these words of Jesus, everyone was amazed, especially Martha, who exclaimed that, since Lazarus was now four days dead, his body must be corrupt.

"Jesus saith to her: Did not I say to thee, that if thou believe, thou shalt see the glory of God?

"They took therefore the stone away. And Jesus lifting up His eyes said: Father, I give Thee thanks that Thou hast heard Me.

"And I knew that Thou hearest Me always; but because of the people who stand about have I said it, that they may believe that Thou hast sent Me.

"When He had said these things, He cried with a loud voice: Lazarus, come forth.

"And presently he that had been dead came forth, bound feet and hands with winding bands; and his face was bound about with a napkin. Jesus said to them: Loose him, and let him go." (St. John xi, 17–44.)

JESUS IN BETHANIA

The Sanhedrin Resolves to Destroy Jesus

St. John the Evangelist, who was present at the raising of Lazarus, and who afterwards heard from the converted Jews all that had been done and said about Jesus and Lazarus, tells us that many of the Jews who were come to Martha and Mary and had seen this which Jesus did, believed in Him; but some of them hurried off to the Sanhedrin and told them the things that Jesus had done. The hatred and envy felt by the ruling party towards Jesus, and their fear of Him, led them to decide at once upon His death.

The Passover was near at hand and many people from all over Judea would soon be in Jerusalem. The enemies of Our Lord feared that these people would believe in Jesus if nothing were done to check His work. Then too they probably feared that He was coming to declare Himself king, that there would be a rebellion, and that Rome, in crushing the outbreak, would take from them their religious freedom, as she had already deprived them of much of their political liberty.

Something must be done to prevent all this. Therefore the chief priests and Pharisees gathered a Great Council against Jesus. It is believed that this was held outside Jerusalem on a high hill, still known as the "Hill of Evil Council."

THE JOURNEYS OF JESUS

QUESTION

Why did the Jews not rejoice in the resurrection of Lazarus?

THE HILL OF EVIL COUNCIL

At the meeting on the Hill of Evil Council the chief priests and Pharisees said: "What do we, for this Man doth many miracles?

"If we let Him alone so, all will believe in Him; and the Romans will come, and take away our place and nation."

As might be expected, there was much disputing at the meeting, when "Caiphas, being the high priest that year, said to them: You know nothing.

"Neither do you consider that it is expedient for you that one man should die for the people, and that the whole nation perish not."

Without knowing it, Caiphas was uttering the will of the Most Holy Trinity. Long ages before it had been decided in the Eternal Council that One should die, not for one nation, but for the whole human race.

The advice of Caiphas did not meet any opposition. "From that day therefore they devised to put Him to death." The friends of Jesus brought word to Him of what had been decided at the Council of the Sanhedrin. Because the time for His death had

JESUS IN BETHANIA

not yet come, Jesus left Jerusalem and "walked no
more openly among the Jews; but He went into a
country near the desert, unto a city that is called
Ephrem, and there He abode with His disciples."
(St. John xi, 47–54.)

QUESTIONS

1. After what miracle did the Jews decide upon putting Jesus to death?

2. Why did Christ become Man?

3. Why did the Jewish priests and Pharisees hate
Jesus?

JESUS RETIRES TO EPHREM

It was probably on hearing of the decision of the
council that Our Saviour decided to retire to Ephrem.
Ephrem is a town sixteen miles north of Jerusalem,
near the borders of Samaria, a lovely place in a
mountainous district. It is in memory of Christ's
retirement to Ephrem that the Church orders images
and crucifixes veiled from Passion Sunday until Holy
Saturday afternoon.

QUESTIONS

1. Locate Ephrem on the map.

2. Why did Christ retire to this place?

3. Who were with Jesus at this time?

4. How do you think He spent the time in this place?

A NINTH JOURNEY
OF JESUS

In this ninth journey, Jesus traveled from Ephrem through northern Samaria and southern Galilee. Thence He went through Perea to Jericho and Bethany, from which place He was to begin His last great journey to Jerusalem.

The principal things to be remembered about this journey are:

> The Healing of the Ten Lepers
> The Coming of the Kingdom of God
> The Judge, the Pharisee, and the Publican
> The Discourse on Christian Marriage
> Christ and Little Children
> The Rich Young Man
> The Parable of the Laborers in the Vineyard
> The Third Prediction of the Passion
> The Ambition of the Two Sons of Zebedee
> The Healing of Two Blind Men
> The Repentance of Zacheus
> The Parable of the Nobleman and the Pounds
> The Banquet in the House of Simon the Leper
> The Praise of Mary

XXV

JESUS IN SAMARIA AND GALILEE

He Heals Ten Lepers

A few weeks before the Passover Jesus left Ephrem, going northward to the frontiers of Samaria and Galilee. While in that neighborhood He performed one of His last miracles,—the healing of ten lepers.

Though lepers were banished from home and friends and were driven far from the cities and towns, they were allowed to associate with other lepers, and even to dwell together. This accounts for the fact that ten lepers came at the same time to the Saviour.

One of these ten was a Samaritan. He and the nine Jews were afflicted with the same loathsome disease. In their common suffering, these unfortunates had forgotten their national and religious hatred.

"And as He entered into a certain town, there met Him ten men that were lepers, who stood afar off;

"And lifted up their voice, saying: Jesus, Master, have mercy on us.

[161]

"Whom when He saw, He said: Go, show yourselves to the priests. And it came to pass, as they went, they were made clean."

Alike they had all suffered; alike they all asked the same favor, received the same command, and were cured at the same time; but how different the conduct of one of these lepers from that of the others after their cure! Nine of the lepers, rejoicing in their renewed health, hurried away without a word of thanks for their miraculous cure. One of them, only one, "when he saw that he was made clean, went back, with a loud voice glorifying God.

"And he fell on his face before His feet, giving thanks: and this was a Samaritan."

The nine Jews had left it to the one Samaritan to throw himself at the feet of Jesus and return gratitude for the miraculous cleansing. Although the Saviour was accustomed to all kinds of neglect, He felt most keenly this act of ingratitude, for while He praised the faith and gratitude of this "stranger," He said to him: "Were not ten made clean? and where are the nine?

"There is no one found to return and give glory to God, but this stranger.

"And He said to him: Arise, go thy way; for thy faith hath made thee whole." (St. Luke xvii, 12–19.)

THE TEN LEPERS

THE JOURNEYS OF JESUS

QUESTIONS

1. Mark on the map the place where the ten lepers met Jesus.

2. Why did Jesus call the Samaritan a "stranger"?

3. When were the lepers cured of their disease?

4. When ill, we pray to God for health. Should we thank Him for continued health?

5. What priest gave his life to serve the lepers of Molokai in the Hawaiian Islands?

THE COMING OF THE KINGDOM OF GOD

The healing of the ten lepers made a deep impression on all who saw the miracle. It likewise attracted the attention of some Pharisees of Galilee. These men, seeing that Jesus still showed mighty power in word and deed, and spoke of the approach of God's Kingdom, yet gave no signs of any royal splendor or magnificence such as they had looked for from Him, asked Him when the Kingdom of God should come.

He answered them and said: "The Kingdom of God cometh not with observation:

"Neither shall they say: Behold here, or behold there. For lo, the Kingdom of God is within you."

Then Jesus said to His disciples: "The days will come, when you shall desire to see one day of the Son of Man; and you shall not see it."

JESUS IN SAMARIA AND GALILEE

He warned them that when the days of suffering
came they were not to heed deceivers who would try
to lead them astray.

"And they will say to you: See here, and see there.
Go ye not after, nor follow them:

"For as the lightning that lighteneth from under
heaven, shineth unto the parts that are under heaven,
so shall the Son of Man be in His day.

"But first He must suffer many things, and be rejected by this generation."

Our Saviour reminded them also that, in the days
of Noe, people, although warned, were careless and
failed to prepare for the great flood that destroyed
all but Noe and his family. "So shall it be also," He
declared, "in the days of the Son of Man."

Likewise was it in the days of Lot, the people ate
and drank, bought and sold, planted and built, and
heeded not God's warning. "And in the day that Lot
went out of Sodom, it rained fire and brimstone from
heaven, and destroyed them all.

"Even thus shall it be in the day when the Son of
Man shall be revealed.

"In that hour, he that shall be on the housetop,
and his goods in the house, let him not go down to
take them away: and he that shall be in the field,
in like manner, let him not return back.

"Remember Lot's wife.

THE JOURNEYS OF JESUS

"Whosoever shall seek to save his life, shall lose it: and whosoever shall lose it, shall preserve it.

"I say to you: in that night there shall be two men in one bed; the one shall be taken, and the other shall be left.

"Two women shall be grinding together: the one shall be taken, and the other shall be left: two men shall be in the field; the one shall be taken, and the other shall be left.

"They answering, say to Him: Where, Lord?

"Who said to them: Wheresoever the body shall be, thither will the eagles also be gathered together." (St. Luke xvii, 20–37.)

St. Ambrose compares the souls of the just to eagles; wherever the Body of the Son of Man shall be, these holy souls shall gather to nourish themselves with His Eucharistic Body and Blood.

QUESTIONS

1. Read in your Bible history the stories of Noe and Lot.

2. Why did Christ mention them in His discourse on this occasion?

3. Quote the answer of Jesus to the Pharisees' question: "When shall the Kingdom of God come?"

4. What do you know about eagles?

5. Find out something about the life of St. Ambrose.

THE JUDGE, THE PHARISEE, AND THE PUBLICAN

The hearts of the disciples were filled with fear of the judgment which Jesus had just revealed to them. To assure them that they need not be taken by surprise, He taught them by means of two parables that they ought "always to pray, and not to faint."

He said: "There was a judge in a certain city, who feared not God, nor regarded man.

"And there was a certain widow in that city, and she came to him, saying: Avenge me of my adversary.

"And he would not for a long time. But afterwards he said within himself: Although I fear not God, nor regard man,

"Yet because this widow is troublesome to me, I will avenge her, lest continually coming she weary me.

"And the Lord said: Hear what the unjust judge saith.

"And will not God revenge His elect who cry to Him day and night: and will He have patience in their regard?

"I say to you, that He will quickly revenge them. But yet the Son of Man, when He cometh, shall He find, think you, faith on earth?"

This parable taught the necessity of prayer. Jesus

[167]

then related another parable, that of the Pharisee and the publican, to teach in what spirit we should pray if we are anxious to obtain our requests.

"And to some who trusted in themselves as just, and despised others, He spoke also this parable:

"Two men went up into the Temple to pray: the one a Pharisee, and the other a publican.

"The Pharisee standing, prayed thus with himself: O God, I give Thee thanks that I am not as the rest of men, extortioners, unjust, adulterers, as also is this publican.

"I fast twice in a week: I give tithes of all that I possess.

"And the publican, standing afar off, would not so much as lift up his eyes towards heaven; but struck his breast, saying: O God, be merciful to me a sinner.

"I say to you, this man went down into his house justified rather than the other: because every one that exalteth himself, shall be humbled: and he that humbleth himself, shall be exalted." (St. Luke xviii, 1–14.)

The prayer of the Pharisee began with thanksgiving to God that he was not sinful like others, and ended with praise of himself; whereas the publican began by acknowledging his sins and ended by asking forgiveness for them.

THE PHARISEE AND THE PUBLICAN

THE JOURNEYS OF JESUS

QUESTIONS

1. What lesson may be taken from the parable of the judge and the widow?

2. What is meant by the second coming of Jesus?

3. What judgment will take place at the second coming of Jesus?

4. Show how these three parables teach that perseverance and humility are qualities of prayer pleasing to God, and that the prayer of the proud is displeasing to Him.

XXVI

JESUS IN JUDEA

He Discourses on Christian Marriage

At the close of His discourse on prayer Jesus left Galilee and came "into the coasts of Judea, beyond Jordan." As usual the crowds flocked to Him, and He taught them, and healed all who were afflicted with diseases. But some Pharisees, wishing to ensnare him, asked: "Is it lawful for a man to put away his wife for every cause?"

Jesus, without answering them directly, said: "Have ye not read, that He Who made man from the beginning, *Made them male and female?*"

And quoting from the Scriptures again, He said: "*For this cause shall a man leave father and mother, and shall cleave to his wife, and they two shall be in one flesh.*

"Therefore now they are not two, but one flesh. What therefore God hath joined together, let no man put asunder."

The Pharisees said: "Why then did Moses command to give a bill of divorce, and to put away?"

To lay bare the deceit of the Pharisees, Jesus replied: "Because Moses by reason of the hardness of your heart permitted you to put away your wives: but from the beginning it was not so." Our Lord then pointed out the sacredness of the married state and declared it to be sinful for a man to leave his wife and marry another woman. (St. Matthew xix, 1–9.)

Leaving the crowds which pressed about Him, Jesus, accompanied by his Apostles, went into His dwelling place. No sooner was He within the house than the Apostles began to question Him about marriage. That the marriage contract must last for life seemed to them a hardship. They therefore said to Him: "If the case of a man with his wife be so, it is not expedient to marry."

Jesus said: "All men take not this word, but they to whom it is given."

These words of Our Lord mean that it requires a special call and a special grace of God to lead a life of virginity. The married state is intended for the great mass of mankind, that they may bring up children in the fear and love of God; but there are some who are specially chosen to lead a single life. They give up the comforts of married life that they may serve God with a greater purity of purpose. (St. Matthew xix, 10–11.)

JESUS IN JUDEA

QUESTIONS

1. What is meant by Christian marriage?

2. What alone can dissolve the bond of Christian marriage?

3. What is a vow?

4. What is meant by a religious life?

5. What people today leave home and everything else for Christ's sake?

CHRIST AND LITTLE CHILDREN

Many mothers, hearing that Jesus was about to leave their neighborhood, were anxious to have Him lay His sacred hands upon their children and bless them.

Jesus loved children and was gladdened at the sight of them. Once before, He had called unto Him a little child and set him in the midst of the Apostles, telling them to be like the child in simplicity and humility.

The Apostles, who were thinking of Our Lord's comfort, did not wish to have the children brought to Him. They thought the little ones would annoy Him. They therefore checked the mothers that brought them. When Jesus saw His chosen Twelve trying to persuade the mothers to take the children away, He rebuked them, and said: "Suffer the little

[173]

children to come unto Me, and forbid them not; for of such is the Kingdom of God.

"Amen I say to you, whosoever shall not receive the Kingdom of God as a little child, shall not enter into it.

"And embracing them, and laying His hands upon them, He blessed them." (St. Mark x, 13–16.)

Since the days of Our Saviour, Holy Mother Church has followed Christ's example in the treatment of children; she makes every sacrifice to instruct them, to preserve their innocence, and to care for the needs of their bodies as well as of their innocent souls. Catholic schools, homes, and hospitals are built and supported by the faithful clergy and people that these little ones may be saved from every danger.

QUESTIONS

1. Why did Jesus love little children?

2. How does the Catholic Church imitate Him in regard to children?

3. Have the faithful any duty to perform in regard to children? If so, what is it?

THE RICH YOUNG MAN

"And behold one came and said to Him: Good Master, what good shall I do that I may have life everlasting?"

[174]

"OF SUCH IS THE KINGDOM OF GOD"

The Gospel of St. Matthew tells us that this inquirer was "a young man," and the Gospel of St. Mark indicates his eagerness, by telling us that he came "running up" to Jesus to ask Him this question.

Jesus replied to him: "Why askest thou Me concerning good? One is good, God. But if thou wilt enter into life, keep the Commandments."

"Which commandments?" asked the young man.

"Jesus said: *Thou shalt do no murder, Thou shalt not commit adultery, Thou shalt not steal, Thou shalt not bear false witness.*

"*Honor thy father and thy mother*: and, *Thou shalt love thy neighbor as thyself.*"

"All these I have kept from my youth," replied the young man, "what is yet wanting to me?"

Jesus, looking upon him, loved him for his goodness and for his earnest desire for holiness. He replied:

"If thou wilt be perfect, go sell what thou hast, and give to the poor, and thou shalt have treasure in heaven: and come follow Me.

"And when the young man had heard this word," says St. Matthew, "he went away sad: for he had great possessions.

"Then Jesus said to His disciples: Amen, I say to you, that a rich man shall hardly enter into the Kingdom of Heaven."

Jesus had often before spoken of riches as a

"HE WENT AWAY SAD: FOR HE HAD GREAT POSSESSIONS"

hindrance to salvation, but the disciples had never seemed to understand the meaning of His words about wealth, and now, as St. Mark tells us, they "were astonished at His words." (St. Matthew xix, 16–23.)

THE DANGERS OF WEALTH

Like an anxious mother speaking to her heedless children, Jesus repeated again what He had just said: "Children, how hard is it for them that trust in riches, to enter into the Kingdom of God?

"It is easier for a camel to pass through the eye of a needle, than for a rich man to enter into the Kingdom of God."

The disciples hearing Jesus, wondered more than before, saying among themselves: "Who then can be saved?"

Jesus replied: "With men it is impossible; but not with God: for all things are possible with God."

Peter, always eager and hasty, interrupted the teaching of Jesus and said: "Behold, we have left all things, and have followed Thee.

"Jesus answering, said: Amen I say to you, there is no man who hath left house or brethren, or sisters, or father, or mother, or children, or lands, for My sake and for the Gospel,

"Who shall not receive an hundred times as much,

JESUS IN JUDEA

now in this time; houses, and brethren, and sisters, and mothers, and children, and lands, with persecutions: and in the world to come life everlasting.

"But many that are first, shall be last: and the last, first." (St. Mark x, 24–31.)

QUESTIONS

1. Are riches in themselves bad?

2. What is the difference between "the poor" and "the poor in spirit"?

3. Which class did Christ call "blessed"?

4. Can people of great worldly wealth be poor in spirit?

5. What promises of reward did Jesus make to those who leave all to follow Him?

6. The rich young man had kept the Commandments from his youth. Why did he go away sorrowful from Jesus?

The Laborers in the Vineyard

So that the Apostles might not take unrighteous pride in their high office of apostolic laborers, and in the great rewards promised them in the life to come, Jesus spoke another parable: "The Kingdom of Heaven is like to an householder, who went out early in the morning to hire laborers into his vineyard.

"And having agreed with the laborers for a penny a day, he sent them into his vineyard.

"And going out about the third hour, he saw others standing in the market place idle.

"And he said to them: Go you also into my vineyard, and I will give you what shall be just.

"And they went their way. And again he went out about the sixth and the ninth hour, and did in like manner.

"But about the eleventh hour he went out and found others standing, and he saith to them: Why stand you here all the day idle?

"They say to him: Because no man hath hired us. He saith to them: Go you also into my vineyard.

"And when evening was come, the lord of the vineyard saith to his steward: Call the laborers and pay them their hire, beginning from the last even to the first.

"When therefore they were come, that came about the eleventh hour, they received every man a penny.

"But when the first also came, they thought that they should receive more: and they also received every man a penny.

"And receiving it they murmured against the master of the house,

"Saying: These last have worked but one hour,

and thou hast made them equal to us, that have borne the burden of the day and the heats.

"But he answering said to one of them: Friend, I do thee no wrong: didst thou not agree with me for a penny?

"Take what is thine, and go thy way: I will also give to this last even as to thee.

"Or, is it not lawful for me to do what I will? is thy eye evil, because I am good?

"So shall the last be first, and the first last. For many are called, but few chosen." (St. Matthew xx, 1–16.)

The Jews made use of the Chaldean method of division of the day, yet like the Romans, they often divided the day into twelve hours and these into four periods each including three hours. The first period commenced at six in the morning; the second about nine; the third at noon; and the fourth at three in the afternoon.

QUESTIONS

1. Can you quote from memory the parable of the laborers in the vineyard?

2. Give the Roman division of the day.

3. Does length of life always mean a better life?

4. Name some saints who died young.

XXVII

JESUS ON THE EAST BANK
OF THE JORDAN

The Third Prediction of the Passion

Jesus continued to instruct His Apostles and to preach to the people, as He went along the eastern bank of the Jordan "going up to Jerusalem: and Jesus went before them, and they were astonished, and following were afraid. And taking again the Twelve, He began to tell them the things that should befall Him."

These were the last days before the paschal feast and many bands of pilgrims on their way to the Holy City met the Saviour and His little group. These pilgrims gathered round Him in large numbers.

It was the month of March, and everything in nature made a setting of beauty for the beloved Master and His friends as they traveled through the country. But the Apostles were in no mood to take pleasure in all this beauty, for they feared what might happen to their Master and to themselves in the city to which they were going. Twice before, Our

Lord had spoken to them of His Passion, but on neither occasion had He told them that He was to hang upon the Cross, nor had He told them in detail of the other sufferings that would come upon Him before the Crucifixion.

Now He said to them: "Behold we go up to Jerusalem, and the Son of Man shall be betrayed to the chief priests, and to the Scribes and ancients, and they shall condemn Him to death, and shall deliver Him to the Gentiles.

"And they shall mock Him, and spit on Him, and scourge Him, and kill Him: and the third day He shall rise again."

These were words of such dreadful meaning that the Apostles could scarcely believe Our Saviour meant that He would suffer such treatment at the hands of His enemies. (St. Mark x, 32–34.)

QUESTIONS

1. Can you tell the three occasions upon which Jesus predicted His Sacred Passion?

2. Why did the Apostles not understand the Saviour's prediction of His Passion?

3. In what way did this third prediction of His Passion differ from the others?

4. Quote the words given in this chapter that foretell the Resurrection of Christ.

[183]

THE JOURNEYS OF JESUS

THE TWO SONS OF ZEBEDEE

"Then came to Him the mother of the sons of Zebedee with her sons, adoring and asking something of Him.

"Who said to her: What wilt thou? She saith to Him: Say that these my two sons may sit, the one on Thy right hand, and the other on Thy left, in Thy Kingdom.

"And Jesus answering, said: You know not what you ask. Can you drink the chalice that I shall drink? They say to Him: We can.

"He saith to them: My chalice indeed you shall drink; but to sit on My right or left hand, is not Mine to give you, but to them for whom it is prepared by My Father."

Their request was not secret enough to be unknown to the other ten, and they "were moved with indignation against the two brethren.

"But Jesus called them to Him, and said: You know that the princes of the Gentiles lord it over them; and they that are the greater, exercise power upon them.

"It shall not be so among you: but whosoever will be the greater among you, let him be your minister:

"And he that will be first among you, shall be your servant.

[184]

JESUS ON THE EAST BANK OF THE JORDAN

"Even as the Son of Man is not come to be ministered unto, but to minister, and to give His life a redemption for many." (St. Matthew xx, 20–28.)

QUESTIONS

1. Which were the places of honor in a king's palace?

2. Who desired these places at the very time when Jesus had spoken of His humiliations, sufferings, and Death?

3. In what way did the sons of Zebedee, St. James and St. John, prove that they could drink the chalice of suffering that Jesus offered them?

XXVIII

JESUS NEAR JERICHO

THE TWO BLIND MEN BY THE WAYSIDE

Many poor people, especially those afflicted with blindness, sat along the wayside begging alms from the crowds who were journeying to the Holy City. When Jesus and His companions had crossed the Jordan and were nearing Jericho, two blind men were sitting by the roadside. Multitudes followed Jesus from town to town. The sounds of the passing multitudes attracted the attention of the blind men. One of them asked what the noise meant. When they heard that it was Jesus of Nazareth passing, both of them "cried out, saying: O Lord, Thou Son of David, have mercy on us."

Their piercing cries kept growing louder and more shrill, so that the multitude rebuked them, telling them to hold their peace. But they only "cried out the more, saying: O Lord, Thou Son of David, have mercy on us."

Touched with pity, "Jesus stood, and called them, and said: What will ye that I do to you?

GIVING SIGHT TO TWO BLIND MEN

"They said to Him: Lord, that our eyes be opened.

"And Jesus having compassion on them, touched their eyes. And immediately they saw, and followed Him." (St. Matthew xx, 29–34.)

QUESTIONS

1. Jesus knew what the blind men desired Him to do for them. Why then did He ask: "What will ye that I do to you?"

2. How did these blind men show their gratitude to Jesus?

XXIX

JESUS IN JERICHO

The Wealth of Jericho

There were still six hours of travel before Jesus could reach Bethania, so He remained overnight in Jericho.

Many glowing accounts are given of the wealth of the inhabitants of Jericho. The country round about produced an abundant harvest of balsam; its fig and palm trees were famous; the dates were of superior quality; the honeybee found there, as nowhere else, a wealth of sweet flowers and plants; and the wheat ripened long before that of any of the other regions of Palestine.

Zacheus Entertains Jesus in his House

Jericho was a paradise for the Roman tax-gatherers, one of whom was Zacheus, a Jew. He was the chief of the publicans and, as such, was hated by the Jews because he had acquired his great wealth by taxing them. Still, he seems to have been a generous and upright man, and he had a very great desire to see Jesus. St. Luke tells the story of Zacheus:

"And entering in, He walked through Jericho.

"And behold, there was a man named Zacheus, who was the chief of the publicans, and he was rich.

"And he sought to see Jesus Who He was, and he could not for the crowd, because he was low of stature.

"And running before, he climbed up into a sycamore tree, that he might see Him; for He was to pass that way.

"And when Jesus was come to the place, looking up, He saw him, and said to him: Zacheus, make haste and come down; for this day I must abide in thy house.

"And he made haste and came down; and received Him with joy.

"And when all saw it, they murmured, saying, that He was gone to be a guest with a man that was a sinner."

No one knows what conversation took place inside the house; we know only the result of the visit. "But Zacheus standing, said to the Lord: Behold, Lord, the half of my goods I give to the poor; and if I have wronged any man of any thing, I restore him fourfold.

JESUS IN JERICHO

"Jesus said to him: This day is salvation come to this house, because he also is a son of Abraham.

"For the Son of Man is come to seek and to save that which was lost." (St. Luke xix, 1–10.)

QUESTIONS

1. Why did the Jews not hold Zacheus in high regard?

2. In what way did Zacheus show the virtue of humility and the sincerity of his repentance?

3. Give in your own words the story of Zacheus.

4. How did Jesus reward Zacheus for his hospitality?

5. Give in your own words the meaning of the last quotation in this chapter.

6. Find out something of the size and appearance of a sycamore tree.

THE NOBLEMAN AND THE POUNDS

When Jesus took leave of Zacheus, He found the crowds eagerly awaiting His coming, for they hoped that He was about to go up to Jerusalem to proclaim there His reign and His Kingdom.

Jesus did not leave them long in ignorance of the nature of His Kingdom. As so often before, He gave them the truth in the form of a parable: "A certain nobleman went into a far country, to receive for himself a kingdom, and to return.

"And calling his ten servants, he gave them ten pounds, and said to them: Trade till I come.

"But his citizens hated him: and they sent an embassage after him, saying: We will not have this man to reign over us.

"And it came to pass, that he returned, having received the kingdom: and he commanded his servants to be called, to whom he had given the money, that he might know how much every man had gained by trading.

"And the first came, saying: Lord, thy pound hath gained ten pounds.

"And he said to him: Well done, thou good servant, because thou hast been faithful in a little, thou shalt have power over ten cities.

"And the second came, saying: Lord, thy pound hath gained five pounds.

"And he said to him: Be thou also over five cities.

"And another came, saying: Lord, behold here is thy pound, which I have kept laid up in a napkin;

"For I feared thee, because thou art an austere man: thou takest up what thou didst not lay down, and thou reapest that which thou didst not sow.

"He saith to him: Out of thy own mouth I judge thee, thou wicked servant. Thou knewest that I was an austere man, taking up what I laid not down, and reaping that which I did not sow:

"And why then didst thou not give my money into the bank, that at my coming, I might have exacted it with usury?

"And he said to them that stood by: Take the pound away from him, and give it to him that hath ten pounds.

"And they said to him: Lord, he hath ten pounds.

"But I say to you, that to every one that hath shall be given, and he shall abound: and from him that hath not, even that which he hath, shall be taken from him.

"But as for those my enemies, who would not have me reign over them, bring them hither, and kill them before me.

"And having said these things, He went before, going up to Jerusalem." (St. Luke xix, 12–28.)

QUESTIONS

1. What special reason had Jesus for giving the parable of the nobleman and the pounds?

2. Why was the servant punished who received but one pound and returned it to his master?

3. What explanation can you give about these pounds?

XXX

JESUS IN BETHANIA

THE SUPPER AT SIMON THE LEPER'S

Jesus, in the company of His disciples, left Jericho and again took the road leading to Jerusalem. He had decided to stop at Bethania before going into the city, so that he might visit Lazarus. St. John says: "Jesus therefore, six days before the Pasch, came to Bethania, where Lazarus had been dead, whom Jesus raised to life.

"And they made Him a supper there: and Martha served: but Lazarus was one of them that were at table with Him."

This supper was given to Christ and His Apostles in the house of Simon the leper, doubtless a friend of Lazarus and his sisters. Many of the people knew that Jesus had come to see Lazarus; so they gathered to catch a glimpse of Him, and also to see Lazarus. Meanwhile, the Pharisees were looking for an opportunity to ensnare Jesus in some plot so as to get rid of Him. And they hated Lazarus because, through him, Jesus had shown His power.

JESUS IN BETHANIA

It was at this supper that Judas Iscariot showed that love of money which, with other base passions, led him to betray his Lord and Master. St. John tells the story in these words: "Mary therefore took a pound of ointment of right spikenard, of great price, and anointed the feet of Jesus, and wiped His feet with her hair; and the house was filled with the odor of the ointment.

"Then one of His disciples, Judas Iscariot, he that was about to betray Him, said:

"Why was not this ointment sold for three hundred pence, and given to the poor?

"Now he said this, not because he cared for the poor; but because he was a thief, and having the purse, carried the things that were put therein." (St. John xii, 1–6.)

JESUS PRAISES MARY'S ACT IN ANOINTING HIM

"Jesus therefore said: Let her alone, that she may keep it against the day of My burial.

"For the poor you have always with you; but Me you have not always." (St. John xii, 7–8.)

St. Mark (xiv, 8–9) records some further words of Our Lord referring to Mary and her loving act: "She hath done what she could: she is come beforehand to anoint My body for the burial.

[195]

"Amen, I say to you, wheresoever this Gospel shall be preached in the whole world, that also which she hath done, shall be told for a memorial of her."

QUESTIONS

1. In what way does Mary's anointing refer to the burial of Jesus?

2. To give alms in charity to the poor, and to build and decorate institutions for God's honor are two works pleasing to God. Which of the two did Mary's act resemble?

3. Why did Christ say: "The poor you have always with you"?

4. Find in your Prayer Book upon which Sunday St. Mark's account of Mary's anointing and Jesus' praising her for her act is read.

BIBLICAL GLOSSARY

A List of the Most Important Names Used in
"The Journeys of Jesus"

Key. făt, fāte, ärm, sofạ, mĕt, mēte, ênough, hēr, novẹl, ĭt, īce, nŏt, nōte, melọn, fŏŏt, fōōd, ŭp, ūse, ûrn, stirrụp.

Andrew (ăn'drōō): one of the twelve Apostles, and the brother of Peter.

Bartholomew (bär thŏl'ô mū): one of the Apostles, thought to be the same as Nathanael.

Beelzebub (bê ĕl'zĕ bŭb): a god worshiped by the Philistines, and hence abhorred by the Jews, by whom he was called the Prince of Devils.

Bethabara (bĕth ăb'ạ rạ), or **Bethany:** a place supposed to be on the east side of the Jordan, between the Dead Sea and the Sea of Galilee.

Bethania (bĕ thā'nĭ ạ), or **Bethany:** a village of Palestine.

Bethsaida (bĕth sā'ĭ dạ): a city on the shore of the Sea of Galilee.

Bethsaida-Julias (jōōl'yụs): the "desert place apart" to which the Saviour invited His Apostles.

Cæsarea-Philippi (sĕs ạ rē'ạ fĭ lĭp'ĭ): the town at the base of Mount Hermon, where Peter made his great profession.

Caiphas (kā'yạ fạs): the high priest at the time of the Crucifixion.

Capharnaum (kạ fär'nâ ụm): a town in Galilee on the north-western shore of the Sea of Galilee.

BIBLICAL GLOSSARY

Corozain (kô rō'zān) : a town in Palestine that was once famous.

Dalmanutha (dăl mạ nū'thạ) : a town of Palestine south of the Sea of Galilee on the left bank of the Jordan.

Decapolis (dĕ kăp'ô lĭs) : a portion of Palestine mainly on the east side of the Jordan ; it contained ten cities.

Dedication (dĕd ĭ kā'shụn), **Feast of:** a Jewish feast commemorating the purification of the Temple after its profanation by Antiochus Epiphanes, a pagan enemy.

Didrachma (dī drăk'mạ) : an old Greek silver coin worth about thirty-three cents.

Ephrem (ē'frĕm) : a town in Palestine into which Jesus withdrew with His disciples before His last entry into Jerusalem.

Esdraelon (ĕs drȧ ē'lŏn), **plain of:** a huge, treeless plain in the form of a triangle, one angle being at Mt. Carmel, one in the hills of Samaria, and the third at Mt. Thabor in Galilee. Many noted battles in the history of the Israelites took place in this plain.

Expiation (ĕks pĭ ā'shụn), **Feast of:** a solemn Jewish day of fast when sacrifices were offered in atonement for sin. Also called the Day of Atonement.

Galilee (găl'ĭ lē) : the most northern of the provinces of Palestine at the time of Christ.

Galilee, Sea of: a lake named from the province of Galilee, twelve or fourteen miles long and six or seven miles wide. Called also Sea of Chinnereth, Lake of Genesareth, and Sea of Tiberias.

Gentile (jĕn'tīl): the name given by the Jews to all who did not know the true God.

Groat (grōt) : an old coin worth about eight cents.

BIBLICAL GLOSSARY

Hebrews (hē'brōōz) : the name given to all the descendants of Jacob. They were also called Israelites and Jews.

James (jāmz) : one of the three favorite Apostles, the brother of John and the son of Zebedee.

James the Lesser: one of the Apostles, the son of Alpheus and Mary.

Jericho (jĕr'ĭ kō) : an ancient city in the valley of the Jordan, about six miles north of the Dead Sea.

Jerusalem (jĕ rōō'sạ lĕm) : the capital of Palestine, thirty-two miles from the Mediterranean and eighteen miles from the river Jordan. The sacred city of the Jewish people.

John: the beloved disciple, son of Zebedee and brother of James.

Jonas (jō'nạs) : a prophet of the Old Law.

Jordan (jôr'dạn) : the only river in Palestine, rising in Mount Hermon and emptying into the Dead Sea.

Judas (jōō'dạs), or **Thaddeus** (thăd'ê ụs) : one of the Apostles, a brother of James the Lesser; also called Jude.

Judas Iscariot (ĭs kăr'ĭ ǫt) : one of the twelve Apostles, the one who betrayed Christ.

Judas Machabeus (măk ạ bē'ụs) : a Jewish patriot who led a revolt of his people against the King of Syria. (See 1 Mach. ii, 4.)

Judea (jōō dē'ạ) : a province of Palestine.

Lazarus (lăz'ạ rụs) : the beggar in Christ's story of the rich man. (See St. Luke xvi, 20.)

Lazarus: the brother of Mary and Martha, raised from the dead by our Divine Lord.

Lebanon (lĕb'ạ nǫn), **Mount:** the great mountain range of Central Syria.

Leontes (lē ŏn'tēz) : the Greek name of a river in northern Palestine.

BIBLICAL GLOSSARY

Levi (lē'vī) : one of the Apostles; also called Matthew; the writer of the First Gospel.

Levites (lē'vīts) : the decendants of Levi, who served the priests in the Temple. The priests were Levites, but they were always descendants of Aaron also.

Magedan (măg'ê dăn), or **Magdala** (măg'dạ lạ) : a town in Galilee, the home of St. Mary Magdalen.

Martha (mär'thạ) : a sister of Lazarus and a friend of our Blessed Lord.

Mary (mā'rĭ) : a sister of Lazarus and Martha and a friend of our Blessed Lord.

Messias (mẹ sī'ạs) : a term applied to Christ as the One sent by God for man's redemption.

Nicodemus (nĭk ỏ dē'mụs) : the Jewish admirer of Jesus who came to see Our Saviour by night. He was a member of the Sanhedrin, but took no part in the condemnation of Christ. He was among those who took the Body of Jesus down from the Cross and laid It in the tomb.

Olivet (ŏl'ĭ vĕt), **Mount:** a noted mountain east of Jerusalem.

Orientals (ỏ rĭ ĕn'tạlz) : natives of the Orient or the East.

Passover (păs'ỏ vẽr) : the principal feast of the Jews, reminding them of the sparing of the families of the Israelites when the destroying angel killed the first-born of Egypt.

Perea (pẽr ē'ạ) : a territory to the east of the Jordan between the Sea of Galilee and the Dead Sea.

Pharisees (făr'ĭ sēz) : a religious sect among the Jews.

Philip (fĭl'ĭp) : an Apostle whose home was in Bethsaida.

Phœnicia (fē nĭsh'ĭ ạ) : a country north of Palestine between the Lebanon Mountains and the Mediterranean.

BIBLICAL GLOSSARY

Sadducees (săd'û sēz) : a religious sect among the Jews.

Sanhedrin (săn'hĕ drĭn) : the great council of the Jews.

Sidon (sī'dǫn) : the oldest city of the Phœnicians, and onę of great riches before it was partly destroyed by the Philistines about 1252 B.C.

Siloe (sĭ lō'ē), **Fountain of:** called also the Pool of Siloe. Just outside the south wall of Jerusalem, where our Blessed Lord gave sight to the man born blind.

Simon the Leper: a Jew of Bethania, at whose house Jesus was entertained when on his way to Jerusalem for the last time.

Simon Peter (sī'mǫn pē'tēr) : the chief of the Apostles, whose name was Simon, afterwards changed to Peter.

Simon Zelotes (zĕ lō'tēz) : one of the twelve Apostles. He is called Zelotes (or the Zealot) to distinguish him from St. Peter, whose original name was Simon.

Synagogue (sĭn'ạ gŏg) : the meeting place of the Jews.

Tabernacles (tăb'ēr nă k'lz), **Feast of the:** one of the three great religious feasts of the Jews.

Thabor (tā'bēr), **Mount:** a picturesque mountain of Palestine, said to be the scene of the Transfiguration of Christ.

Thomas (tŏm'ạs) : one of the twelve Apostles, also called Didymus.

Tyre (tīr) : a very rich and powerful city whose wickedness had become proverbial among the Jews at the time of Christ.

www.ingramcontent.com/pod-product-compliance
Lightning Source LLC
LaVergne TN
LVHW011226080426
835509LV00005B/338